Linda Everett & Richard Perry

Retro Breakfast

Memorable Meals Morning, Noon, or Night

COLLECTORS PRESS

PORTLAND, OREGON

Book Design: Wade Daughtry, Collectors Press, Inc.
Editor: Aimee Stoddard

Library of Congress Cataloging-in-Publication Data

Everett, Linda, 1946-
 Retro breakfast : memorable meals morning, noon, or night / by Linda Everett and Richard Perry.-- 1st American ed.
    p. cm. -- (Retro series)
Includes index.
 ISBN 1-888054-87-5 (hardcover : alk. paper)
 1. Breakfasts. 2. Cookery. I. Perry, Richard, 1960- II. Title. III. Series.
 TX733.E94 2004
 641.5'2--dc22
                    2003019060

Printed in Singapore

9 8 7 6 5 4 3 2 1

Collectors Press books are available at special discounts for bulk purchases, premiums, and promotions. Special editions, including personalized inserts or covers, and corporate logos, can be printed in quantity for special purposes. For further information contact: Special Sales, Collectors Press, Inc., P.O. Box 230986 Portland, OR 97281. Toll free: 1-800-423-1848.

Retro Breakfast is part of the *Retro* Series by Collectors Press, Inc.

For a free catalog write: Collectors Press, Inc., P.O. Box 230986, Portland, OR 97281.
Toll free: 1-800-423-1848 or visit our website at: collectorspress.com.

Contents

Introduction

The sun peeks over a calendar-perfect picture in the heartland of America. Smoke drifts out of the chimney as Grandma stokes the huge Monarch wood stove, and soon the delightful smells of honest, rib-stickin' breakfast foods waft throughout the farmhouse. With a yawn, the family throw aside their cozy quilts and sniff the chilly air filled with promises of griddle cakes, ham, rich brown eggs, biscuits n' gravy, bowls of oatmeal with thick cream, and strong coffee. Hard work and long days on the farm called for hearty fuel for the body.

Move ahead to the 1950s and the stove is a shiny Westinghouse gas. It's Sunday morning, and Mom is whipping up one of great-grandma's prized recipes to cook on her electric waffle iron. Fresh orange juice is now the norm, and the coffee is made in a chrome percolator instead of boiled with eggshells on the back of the old wood stove. The weekday breakfast embraces plastic bowls of prepackaged Cheerios or Wheaties served with milk dropped off on your front porch and not from a warm bovine named Mable. Gadgets abound and modern is the buzzword for every Formica-festooned kitchen. Still, Mom is typically stay-at-home, and pancakes, omelets, or other breakfast favorites haven't necessarily become a thing of the past.

These days, much of rural and middle America continues to start the day with the nourishing basics of yesteryear. But, many others have let the best and most important meal of the day slip into the mediocrity of a naked piece of toast with a slurp of instant coffee, or maybe a bowl of microwaved, counterfeit cereal complete with artificial flavor, color, and don't forget the preservatives!

Bring back the delight of plopping down a platter full of fluffy pancakes in front of your kids, pushing over an accompanying array of homemade fruity syrups and jams. Then soak up the huge smiles. Set a delectable omelet or serving of breakfast casserole on the table to comments like, "I remember my Mom making that!" or "Is this Grandma's recipe?" Or consider one of Great Aunt Ida's flowered plates heaped high with mouth-watering biscuits that have never seen the fluorescent glow of a supermarket case. Pop open a few of those fine biscuits, slap on butter and jelly made by loving hands, and let yourself coast on back to the era of comfort food. Consider starting a tradition, or breathe life back into a fondly remembered Sunday ritual, of a breakfast that holds warmhearted memories and creates new ones.

Cackle 'N' Crow

Egg Dishes

The old proverb about which came first — the chicken or the egg — surely didn't come from homestead folk. The scrawny, half-wild little hens worked their way across America, hauled along in handmade coops on bumpy wagons, pecking away on hardscrabble ground. Many a pioneer wife earned a few pennies by selling eggs or bartering them for a bag of flour.

Big, rich, brown eggs from huge, fat, Rhode Island Red hens became the steady diet for many families. Little kids were often given the chore of gathering the daily ration of eggs, risking a nasty pecking as they reached cautiously under the testy biddies.

Since the 1940s, the noble egg switched from brown glories to mass-produced ghostly white from chickens who never got to chase a fat bug or scratch in the dust. Nevertheless, eggs are still the underpinning of a wonderful array of breakfast staples and delights. These days, the know-it-alls inform us it isn't such a terrible sin to indulge in eggs, as long as it's in moderation. So, go ahead and enjoy one of Mother Nature's most versatile offerings.

OMELETS

Shepherd's Omelet

2 MEDIUM ONIONS, CHOPPED
1 MEDIUM SWEET GREEN BELL PEPPER, THINLY SLICED
1 MEDIUM SWEET RED BELL PEPPER, THINLY SLICED
1 SMALL CLOVE GARLIC, MINCED
3 TBLSPS OLIVE OIL
4 MEDIUM RIPE TOMATOES, CHOPPED
1 TSP SALT
1/4 TSP COARSELY GROUND BLACK PEPPER
1/2 CUP HAM, CHOPPED
3 TBLSPS BUTTER
8 EGGS, LIGHTLY BEATEN
2 TBLSPS FRESH PARSLEY, CHOPPED

In a medium skillet, lightly sauté the onions, peppers, and garlic in olive oil until tender but not browned. Add the tomatoes and cook for 5 minutes over low heat. Add in the salt, pepper, and ham and cook until most of liquid is gone, about 10 minutes. In a separate large skillet or omelet pan, melt butter. Pour in eggs. Cook over low heat, raising edge of eggs with your spatula and allowing uncooked egg to run under. When eggs are almost set, remove from heat and spread vegetable mixture over the top. Return to low heat. Use spatula to fold over in half. Sprinkle parsley over top. Cut into wedges and serve hot.

Serves 4 to 6

Iowa Break O' Dawn Omelet

6 EGGS
1/2 CARTON (1 PINT) COTTAGE CHEESE
1/2 TSP SALT
1/4 TSP COARSELY GROUND BLACK PEPPER
2 TBLSPS FRESH CHOPPED CHIVES
1 TBLSP BUTTER

In a medium bowl, beat together the eggs, cottage cheese, salt, pepper, and chives. Melt the butter in a large skillet. Pour in the egg mixture and cook over low heat until firm and lightly browned on the bottom. Flip over in half with your spatula or place under a medium broiler and brown top. Serve hot.

Serves 4

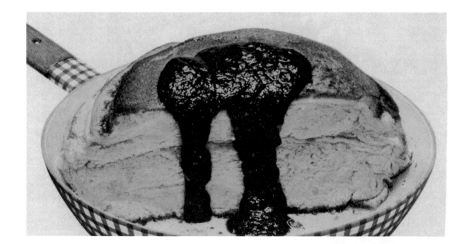

Tuscany Omelet

2 TBLSPS OLIVE OIL
1 MEDIUM CLOVE GARLIC, MINCED
1 SMALL ONION, CHOPPED
6 EGGS
4 TBLSPS PARMESAN CHEESE, GRATED
1/2 TSP SALT
1/4 TSP COARSELY GROUND BLACK PEPPER
1 CUP ZUCCHINI, SLICED AND COOKED UNTIL JUST TENDER
1 MEDIUM RIPE TOMATO, CHOPPED
2 TBLSPS FRESH PARSLEY, CHOPPED
1/4 CUP PARMESAN CHEESE, GRATED

In a large skillet, heat the olive oil and sauté garlic and onion until tender.
Remove and drain on paper towels. Keep warm. In a medium bowl, beat
together the eggs, 4 tablespoons Parmesan cheese, salt, and pepper.
Pour eggs into skillet. Add in garlic, onion, zucchini, and tomato. Cover
and cook over low heat until set. Fold over and sprinkle with the parsley
and extra cheese.

Serves 3 to 4

Okanogan Omelet

1/4 CUP BROWN SUGAR, PACKED
1 TBLSP CORNSTARCH
3/4 CUP COLD WATER, DIVIDED
2 TSP LEMON JUICE
3 LARGE APPLES, PEELED, CORED, AND CUT INTO 1/2-INCH THICK SLICES
1/4 CUP COOKED SAUSAGE
4 TBLSPS BUTTER OR MARGARINE
4 EGGS, SEPARATED
1/4 TSP SALT
1/4 CUP GRATED SHARP CHEDDAR CHEESE

To make apple filling:

In a small saucepan, combine brown sugar and cornstarch. Over medium high heat stir in 2/3 cup water, and lemon juice. Stir constantly until mixture is thick. Add in apples, cover, turn down heat to low and simmer for about 5 minutes or until apples are tender. Stir in the sausage and 2 tablespoons butter. Stir until sausage is hot. Remove from heat and keep warm.

To make omelet:

Preheat oven to 325 degrees.

In a medium bowl, beat egg whites until frothy. Add in rest of the water and salt. Continue beating until whites become stiff. In a separate bowl, beat the yolks until they turn lemon colored. Gently fold yolks into beaten whites. Heat the last tablespoon of butter in a cast iron or other ovenproof skillet. When skillet is hot, but not smoking, pour in egg mixture and spread evenly over skillet, pushing sides up to form a low wall. Bake for 8 to 10 minutes or until butter knife poked in center comes out clean. Loosen sides of omelet with your spatula and score omelet across center. Set aside 1/2 cup of the apple filling. Pour remaining filling across center of omelet and fold over. Pour reserved filling over top. Sprinkle the sharp cheese over this. Serve with homemade biscuits, bread, or cornbread.

Serves 4

Seaside Café's #1 Omelet

5 TBLSPS BUTTER, DIVIDED
1 MEDIUM ONION, MINCED
1 MEDIUM CLOVE GARLIC, MINCED
1/4 CUP SWEET GREEN PEPPER, CHOPPED
2 TBLSPS ALL-PURPOSE FLOUR
2/3 CUP MILK
1/2 CUP PLUS 2 TBLSPS CREAM, DIVIDED
3/4 TSP SALT, DIVIDED
1/2 TSP BLACK PEPPER, DIVIDED
2 TBLSPS DRY SHERRY
1 1/2 CUPS COOKED SEAFOOD (CRAB, SHRIMP, SCALLOPS, LOBSTER, ETC.)
8 EGGS
4 TBLSPS GRATED PARMESAN CHEESE

In a large skillet, melt 1 tablespoon of the butter and sauté onion and garlic until tender. Add green pepper and continue cooking until tender. Remove and set aside. Melt 2 more tablespoons of butter in a saucepan and stir in the flour until thick. Slowly add milk and 1/2 cup cream, stirring constantly until smooth. Season with 1/2 tsp. salt and 1/4 tsp. pepper. Add the onion mixture, sherry, and seafood to the sauce and cook over low just until heated through. In a small bowl, beat together the eggs, cream, and remaining salt and pepper. Melt the last 2 tablespoons butter in a large skillet and pour in eggs. Cook over low heat until just set. Pour half the seafood mixture over omelets and fold in half. Remove to a platter and pour remaining seafood mixture over top and sprinkle with Parmesan cheese.

Serves 4

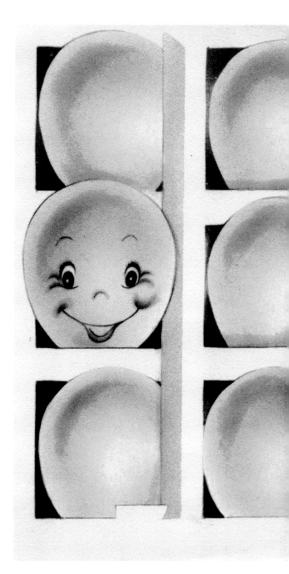

Bunny Hollow Farm Omelet

2 TBLSPS BUTTER, DIVIDED
1 SMALL TOMATO, CHOPPED (ABOUT 1/4 CUP)
1 SMALL CLOVE GARLIC, MINCED
1 TSP FRESH PARSLEY, CHOPPED
3 EGGS, WELL BEATEN
1/2 TSP SALT
1/4 TSP COARSELY GROUND BLACK PEPPER

In a medium skillet, melt the butter and sauté the tomato, garlic, and parsley over low heat for about 5 minutes. Remove from skillet, set aside, and keep warm. Melt the second tablespoon of butter in the skillet or an omelet pan, pour in the eggs, and sprinkle on the salt and pepper. Cook over medium heat, raising edge of omelet to let uncooked portion flow underneath. When the omelet is almost set, spoon on the tomato mixture and fold. Serve hot.

Serves 1

Colorado's Best Omelet

2 TBLSPS BUTTER, DIVIDED
1/2 CUP FRESH MUSHROOMS, THINLY SLICED
1/4 CUP COOKED HAM, CHOPPED
3 EGGS
1 TBLSP COLD WATER
1/2 TSP SALT
1/8 TSP WHITE PEPPER

In a small skillet, melt 1 tablespoon of butter and sauté mushrooms over medium heat for about 3 minutes. Add in the ham and stir well. Cook for another 2 minutes, remove from pan, and keep warm. In a small bowl, beat together the eggs, water, salt, and pepper. In the same skillet or an omelet pan, melt the second tablespoon butter and pour in egg mixture. Cook over medium heat, raising edges with a spatula to let uncooked portion flow underneath. As the omelet sets, spoon over the mushrooms and ham and fold over.

Serves 1

Santa Barbara Omelet

3 TBLSPS BUTTER OR OIL, DIVIDED
3 TBLSPS SWEET GREEN BELL PEPPER, CHOPPED
1/4 CUP SWEET ONION, CHOPPED (MAUI, WALLA WALLA, OR VIDALIA ARE GOOD)
1 LARGE TOMATO, PEELED AND CHOPPED
4 TBLSPS CELERY, CHOPPED
1/2 CUP FRESH MUSHROOMS, THINLY SLICED
1 TSP SALT, DIVIDED
1/4 TSP CAYENNE PEPPER
5 EGGS, SEPARATED
1/8 TSP BLACK PEPPER
5 TBLSPS HOT WATER
1/2 CUP SHARP CHEDDAR CHEESE

In a medium skillet, melt 2 tablespoons butter and sauté the green pepper and onion until tender. Add in the tomato, celery, mushrooms, 1/2 of the salt, and Cayenne pepper. Cook over low heat, stirring occasionally, until tomato is tender, about 5 minutes. In a medium bowl, beat together the egg yolks until thick and lemon colored; add the second salt, pepper, Cayenne, and hot water. Beat the egg whites until stiff and fold into egg yolks. Melt remaining 1 tablespoon butter in a hot, battered heavy skillet or omelet pan and pour in egg mixture. Cook over low heat until omelet is very lightly browned on the bottom. Place in a 350 degree oven for about 10 minutes or until center of omelet springs back when touched. Spoon tomato mixture over omelet. Sprinkle cheese over all. Fold in half and cut into wedges.

Serves 4 to 5

Omelet Shortcake

6 EGGS, SEPARATED
3/4 TSP SALT
1/4 TSP BLACK PEPPER
1 TBLSP SWEET ONION, GRATED
3 TBLSPS FLOUR
2 TBLSPS FRESH PARSLEY, MINCED
1 CUP COOKED CHOPPED CHICKEN, SHRIMP, DRIED CHIPPED BEEF, OR YOUR FAVORITE CHEESE.
2 CUPS WHITE SAUCE (SEE RECIPE ON PAGE 23)

Preheat oven to 350 degrees.

Grease two 8-inch cake layer pans; warm in oven. Using your electric mixer, beat the egg whites with salt until stiff but still shiny. Set aside. Beat egg yolks until well mixed. Add in the pepper, onion, flour, and parsley. Beat until thick. Fold in egg whites. Divide mixture evenly into the 2 pans. Spread out and bake for 15 minutes or until butter knife poked in center comes out clean. Combine your choice of chicken, etc., with the white sauce. Invert one layer of omelet out of its pan onto a nice plate. Spread top with 1/2 cup of the topping. Invert second layer on top of this. Cut into wedges at table and offer remaining sauce to spoon over each serving.

Serves 6

Herb Garden Omelet

6 EGGS
4 TBLSPS CREAM, DIVIDED
1 1/2 TBLSPS BUTTER
2 TBLSPS FRESH PARSLEY, CHOPPED
2 TBLSPS FRESH TARRAGON, CHOPPED
1 TBLSP FRESH CHIVES, CHOPPED
1 TBLSP FRESH BASIL, CHOPPED

In a medium bowl, beat together the eggs and 2 tablespoons cream. Melt butter in a large skillet. Pour in egg mixture and cook over low heat. When the eggs are partially set, drizzle the remaining 2 tablespoons cream over and sprinkle on the parsley, tarragon, chives, and basil. Cover and continue cooking until solid but not dry. Fold over and serve.

Serves 3 to 4

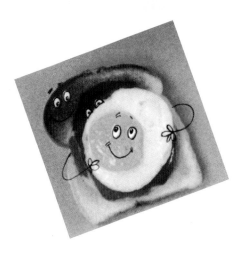

You get eggs like this every time
in the Sunbeam set at 300°

You get the perfect
Controlled Heat →
for more delicious food by
simply setting this dial

Omelet from Woo Ling's Café

4 EGGS, SEPARATED
1/4 TSP WHITE PEPPER
1 1/4 CUP WATER, DIVIDED
1/4 TSP SALT
1/4 TSP CREAM OF TARTAR
6 TBLSPS BUTTER, DIVIDED
1/4 CUP SOY SAUCE
1/4 CUP BROWN SUGAR, FIRMLY PACKED
2 TBLSPS VINEGAR
2 TBLSPS CORNSTARCH
1/2 TSP DRY MUSTARD
1/2 CUP FRESH OR FROZEN SNOW PEAS
1/2 CUP WATER CHESTNUTS, CHOPPED
1/4 CUP SWEET RED BELL PEPPER, CUT IN STRIPS
1/4 CUP SWEET GREEN BELL PEPPER, CUT IN STRIPS
1 1/4 CUPS SHREDDED CHEDDAR CHEESE

Preheat oven to 325 degrees.

In a small bowl, beat egg yolks and white pepper until eggs become thick and lemon colored. In a separate bowl, beat egg whites with 1/4 cup water, salt and cream of tartar. Whites should be stiff but not dry. Fold yolks into whites. Melt 2 tablespoons butter in a medium-sized, oven- proof skillet and pour in egg mixture. Cook over low heat until fluffy and lightly brown on bottom, about 5 minutes. Bake for 12 to 15 minutes or until butter knife inserted in center comes out clean. In a medium saucepan, heat the 1 cup water with soy sauce, brown sugar, vinegar, cornstarch, and dry mustard. Cook over medium heat, stirring constantly, until thickened, about 5 minutes. Remove from heat and stir in second 2 tablespoons of butter. Stir until butter is melted. Add in pea pods, water chestnuts, and bell peppers. Keep warm. Remove omelet to a warm platter and sprinkle 1 cup of the cheese on one half of the omelet. Fold in half and spoon 1/2 cup sauce over top. Sprinkle with remaining 1/2 cup cheese and serve with reserved sauce.

Serves 4

Independence, Kansas, Ham N' Eggs

1/2 CUP COOKED HAM, CUT IN BITE-SIZED PIECES
4 EGGS
4 TBLSPS LIGHT CREAM
1/2 TSP SALT
1/4 TSP COARSELY GROUND BLACK PEPPER
2 TBLSPS BUTTER, MELTED
1/2 CUP BREADCRUMBS

Preheat oven to 400 degrees.

Lightly grease 4 ramekins or other small baking dishes. Divide ham between each ramekin, lining the bottom of each. Crack and egg on top of the ham in each ramekin. Drizzle each with 1 tablespoon of the cream and season with salt and pepper. In a small bowl, mix melted butter with breadcrumbs and sprinkle on top of eggs in each dish. Bake for 8 minutes. Serve with homemade biscuits (see pages 74-101) and offer fruit alongside.

Serves 4

EGGS

Pasadena Eggs

Before walking the two blocks from Linda's grandmother's house to Colorado Boulevard to watch the famous Rose Parade, Grandma would serve creamed eggs with her famous biscuits. See page 76 for the biscuit recipe.

6 HARD-BOILED EGGS, SLICED
2 CUPS WHITE SAUCE (SEE PAGE 23)
1/2 TSP SALT
1/4 TSP COARSELY GROUND BLACK PEPPER
1/4 TSP GARLIC POWDER
2 TBLSPS FRESH PARSLEY, CHOPPED

Over low heat or in microwave, heat eggs in the white sauce. Gently stir in salt, pepper, and garlic powder. Spoon over split biscuits, English muffins, or toast. Sprinkle with parsley.

Serves 6

Huevos a Caballo (Eggs on Horseback)

4 RIPE TOMATOES, CHOPPED
1 SMALL CLOVE GARLIC, CRUSHED
1 SMALL ONION, CHOPPED
2 TBLSPS BUTTER, DIVIDED
2 SWEET RED OR YELLOW BELL PEPPERS
8 EGGS, BEATEN
4 TORTILLAS
4 SLICES CHEESE, TRY PEPPER JACK OR JALAPENO FOR A CHANGE
2 MEDIUM AVOCADOS, PEELED AND CHOPPED

Simmer together the tomatoes, garlic, and onion until they thicken, about 10 minutes. In a skillet, melt 1 tablespoon butter and sauté peppers until tender; set aside. Fry the eggs to just done. Remove peppers from skillet and keep warm. Melt the second tablespoon of butter in the skillet and fry each of the tortillas until lightly browned. Drain on paper towels. Lay a tortilla on a plate, place two cooked eggs on top. Top this with a slice of cheese, a sprinkle of sautéed pepper, then avocado.

Serves 4

Oaxaca (wah-hah-cah) Coast

2 CUPS CANNED TOMATOES, CHOPPED
1/2 SMALL ONION, CHOPPED
1 TBLSP FRESH CILANTRO, MINCED, OR 1 TSP DRIED
1 TSP DRIED GROUND CHILI POWDER
1 SMALL CAN CHOPPED GREEN CHILIES, DRAINED
1 TSP SUGAR
3/4 TSP SALT
2 TBLSP BUTTER
2 TBLSP ALL-PURPOSE FLOUR
3 CUPS COOKED LONG-GRAIN RICE (1 CUP UNCOOKED)
6 EGGS
1/2 CUP GRATED SHARP CHEDDAR CHEESE
1/2 CUP CRUMBLED CORN CHIPS (LIKE FRITOS)

Preheat oven to 350 degrees.

In a large saucepan, simmer the tomatoes, onion, cilantro, chili powder, green chilies, sugar, and salt for about 10 minutes. (Some people prefer to strain this mixture, but the chunks of tomato and onion are nice for texture.) Melt butter in a separate pan and blend in flour. Pour in tomato mixture and cook over medium heat, stirring constantly until mixture thickens. Grease or butter a shallow 2 1/2-quart casserole dish and spread uncooked rice over bottom. Use a large serving spoon to press an indentation for the eggs. Break an egg into each of these hollows and gently pour tomato mixture over all. Sprinkle crumbled chips over all followed by the cheese (for a change try Pepper Jack). Bake for 25 minutes or until eggs and rice are done. Offer sour cream and guacamole or avocado slices as toppings.

Serves 6

Yodeler Pie

1 1/2 CUPS GRATED SWISS CHEESE
   (TRY OTHER VARIETIES OF CHEESE, TOO)
1 TSP ONION, MINCED
4 EGGS
1 TSP SALT
1 CUP HEAVY CREAM
PASTRY FOR 8-INCH PIE SHELL

Preheat oven to 400 degrees.

In a large bowl, combine together cheese, onion, eggs, salt, and cream. Pour into pie shell. Bake for 10 minutes, then turn down heat to 300. Bake 40 minutes more or until butter knife stuck in center comes out clean. If pie crust looks like it's getting too brown, cover with a strip of aluminum foil for the last few minutes.

Serves 4 to 6

South Dakota Spring Eggs

The white sauce:
2 TBLSPS BUTTER
2 TBLSPS ALL-PURPOSE FLOUR
1 CUP COLD MILK
1/4 TSP SALT

In a small skillet or saucepan, melt butter over low heat. Add in flour and stir until smooth and slightly nutty smelling. Slowly add in the cold milk and whisk over medium heat until thick, stirring frequently. Stir in salt. Keep warm.

The White Sauce

The eggs:
4 SLICES GOOD WHITE BREAD, TOASTED
1 TBLSP SWEET ONION, MINCED
1 TBLSP SWEET RED OR YELLOW BELL PEPPER, MINCED
1/4 CUP GRATED SHARP CHEESE OR SPREADABLE CHEESE (TRY DIFFERENT FLAVORS -- THE SMOKY IS GREAT!)
4 EGGS

While toast is hot, sprinkle or spread on cheese. Keep warm. In a shallow saucepan, poach eggs by bringing water to barely simmering and gently crack egg into water without covering. Cook about 11 to 12 minutes, remove with slotted spoon, and dab bottom of spoon with paper towel to absorb excess water. Meanwhile, stir onion and sweet pepper in white sauce. Place one egg on each piece of toast and pour hot white sauce over all. You might offer fresh chopped tomato to top it off.

Serves 4

Cool Morning Breakfast

3 TBLSPS BUTTER
1 SMALL SWEET ONION, CHOPPED
2 CUPS CUBED BREAD, GOOD HOMEMADE IS BEST (SEE PAGE 88)
8 EGGS
1/4 CUP MILK
1 TSP SALT
1/2 TSP FRESHLY GROUND BLACK PEPPER
2 TBLSPS FRESH CHIVES, CHOPPED

In a large skillet, melt the butter over medium heat and sauté the onion and bread cubes. Onion should be tender and crumbs should be golden brown. Takes about 8 minutes. Stir often. Meanwhile, beat the eggs, milk, salt, and pepper in a bowl. When the onion/bread mixture is done, pour the egg mixture into the skillet and cook like scrambled eggs, scraping skillet and folding the eggs as they cook. Cook until set. Divide into 4 servings and sprinkle chives over each. (Optional: try topping it all off with a little grated sharp cheddar cheese – yum!)

Serves 4

Red Rabbit

2 TBLSPS BUTTER OR SHORTENING
1/2 SMALL ONION, CHOPPED
1/2 SMALL GREEN BELL PEPPER, CHOPPED
1/3 CUP CELERY, CHOPPED
1 1/2 TBLSPS ALL-PURPOSE FLOUR
1 1/2 CUPS CANNED TOMATOES, CHOPPED STYLE
1/2 TSP SALT
1 1/2 CUPS GRATED SHARP CHEESE (OR YOUR FAVORITE)
2 EGGS, WELL BEATEN
4 SLICES GOOD BREAD, TOASTED

In a heavy skillet, melt the butter and sauté
onion, green pepper, and celery. Cook until
tender. Blend in flour. Add in tomatoes and salt.
Cook over low heat until mixture is thickened.
Stir often. Remove from heat and stir in cheese
until melted. Pour a small amount of the sauce
into eggs then pour back into tomato/cheese.
Return to medium-low heat and cook until
thick. Serve over toast.

Serves 4

Whole Eggs... Freshly Broken

Toad-in-a-Hole

8 SLICES THICK, GOOD WHITE BREAD (HOMEMADE IS GREAT)
8 STRIPS BACON
8 LARGE EGGS
1/2 TSP SALT
1/4 TSP FRESHLY GROUND BLACK PEPPER

Use a 2-inch cookie or biscuit cutter to cut a hole out of the center of each slice of bread. Set aside the cutout holes. Fry bacon in a large skillet until crisp, about 7 or 8 minutes. Drain on paper towels and keep warm. Drain off all but 1/4-inch of the bacon grease from the pan. Return skillet to medium heat and add in as many bread slices as will comfortably fit. Break an egg in each hole and cook until the egg whites are set, about 1 minute. Take your spatula and carefully flip over the bread/eggs. Cook until done to your liking; an additional 1 minute for "over easy," 2 to 3 minutes more for firm. Bread should be lightly toasted on both sides. Season with salt and pepper. Toast the cutout rounds and serve 2 "toads" to each person, balancing the rounds over hole so it looks like the egg is hiding. (Okay, so use your imagination!) Serve with 2 slices of bacon alongside.

Serves 4

27

RANCH BREAKFAST

Side By Side

Hash Browns 'N' Side Dishes

When you serve those delectable eggs, don't leave them sitting there lonely and incomplete. Fill up that empty space on your plate with one of these companionable side dishes. Think of apples as a new and particularly perfect accompaniment. Why not try them alongside those classic, crispy-edged hash browns for a double dip of taste bud wonder?

Real Hash Browns

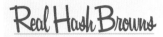

4 MEDIUM-SIZED POTATOES, BOILED UNTIL TENDER AND COOLED
 OR 1 15-OUNCE CAN POTATOES
1 MEDIUM ONION, FINELY CHOPPED
3 TBLSPS BUTTER
1 TSP SALT
1/4 TSP COARSELY GROUND BLACK PEPPER

Dice the potatoes and mix with onion. Heat the butter in a heavy skillet. Add in the potato/onion mixture, salt, and pepper. Cook over medium heat until lightly browned and crispy. Remove.

Serves 4

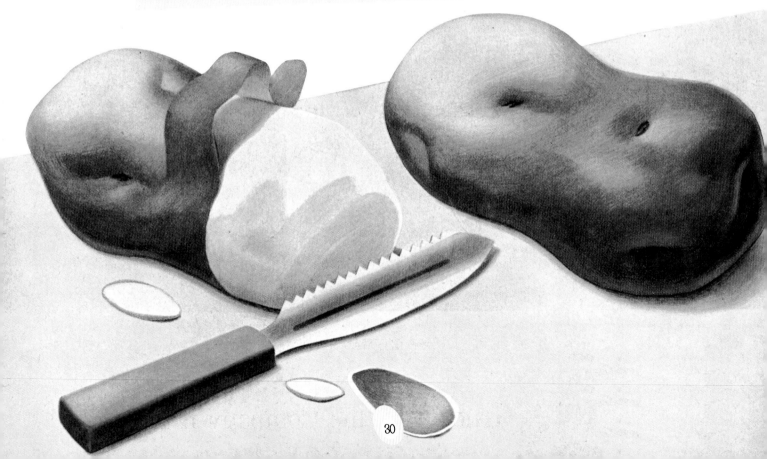

30

Breakfast with a bonus!

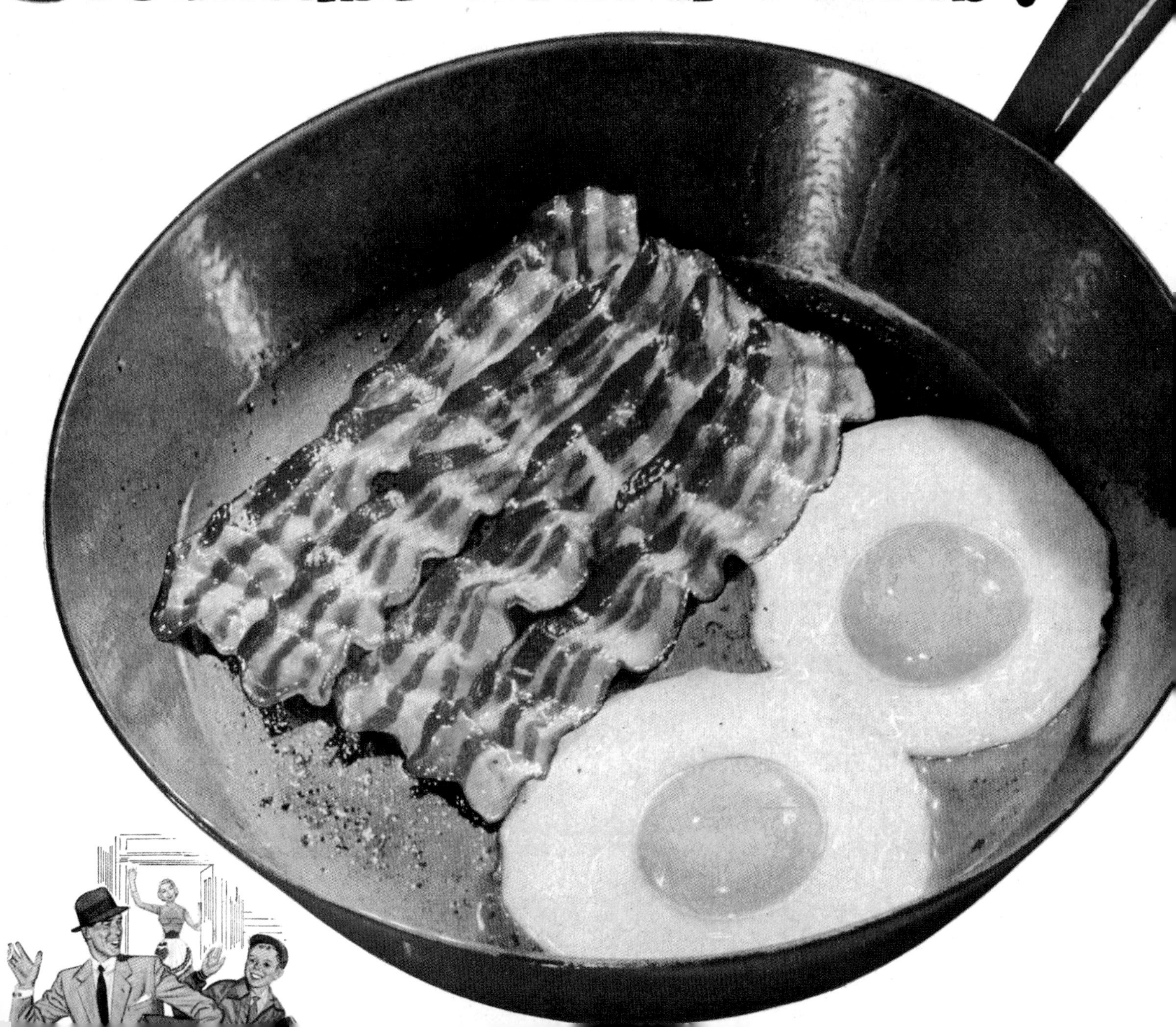

Connecticut Yank Side Dish

3 TBLSPS BUTTER
3 LARGE, FIRM SWEET/TART APPLES, LIKE CORTLAND OR GRANNY
   SMITH. PEELED, CORED, SLICED.
3 LARGE SWEET POTATOES, COOKED, PEELED, SLICED
1/2 CUP GOOD MAPLE SYRUP

Preheat oven to 350 degrees.

In a medium skillet, melt 2 tablespoons butter and
sauté apple slices over medium heat until tender. Butter
a 9 x 9-inch baking dish and alternate layer of sweet
potatoes with apple slices. Dot with remaining
tablespoon butter and pour syrup over all. Bake for
about 35 minutes.

Serves 4 to 6

Portugee Creek Potatoes

2 LARGE BAKING POTATOES, COOKED (SEE BELOW)
1 TSP SALT, DIVIDED
2 TBLSP BUTTER
4 GREEN ONIONS, CHOPPED
1/2 CUP COOKED HAM, CHOPPED
1/2 TSP GARLIC, MINCED
1/2 CUP FRESH MUSHROOMS, WASHED AND THINLY SLICED
1/2 TSP SALT
1/4 TSP BLACK PEPPER

Boil the potatoes in salted water until tender. Drain, peel, and coarsely chop. In a large heavy skillet, melt butter and add in potatoes. Cook over medium heat for 5 to 7 minutes, stirring occasionally until browned. Add in onions, ham, garlic, and mushrooms and continue cooking for 2 minutes longer. Season with salt and pepper and serve hot.

Serves 4

Lulu's Café Home Fries

4 MEDIUM POTATOES, WASHED AND PEELED
1/4 CUP BUTTER
1/2 TSP ONION SALT
1/4 TSP GARLIC POWDER
1/2 TSP SALT
1/4 TSP COARSELY GROUND BLACK PEPPER

Slice potatoes 1/8-inch thick and soak in cold water for 10 minutes. Drain on paper towels and pat dry. Heat butter in heavy skillet. Add in potatoes, onion salt, garlic powder, salt, and pepper. Fry over medium heat until potatoes are tender and browned. Stir gently and often to avoid sticking.

Serves 4

FLOUR

Best call for Breakfast

Miz Daisy's Fried Green Tomatoes

3 MEDIUM-SIZED, FIRM GREEN TOMATOES
3 TBLSPS ALL-PURPOSE FLOUR
1/2 TSP SALT
1/4 TSP COARSELY GROUND BLACK PEPPER
4 TBLSPS BUTTER

Wash tomatoes and slice 1/2-inch thick, pat dry with paper towels. In a small bowl, mix together the flour, salt, and pepper. Melt butter in a heavy skillet. Dip tomatoes into flour mixture and place in single layer in butter. Cover pan, reduce heat, and cook for 10 minutes. Remove cover, increase heat, and brown the slices on both sides. Drain on paper towels. Serve hot.

Serves 4

You're looking "CLOSE-UP" at a new breakfast experience!

New Hampshire Fried Apples

This recipe is more than 100 years old.

2 TBLSPS BUTTER
3 TBLSPS SUGAR
2 TBLSPS (PREFERABLY LIGHT) MOLASSES
1 TBLSP WATER
6 SWEET/TART APPLES, CUT INTO EIGHTHS, CORED —
    MCINTOSH, JONATHANS, OR FUJI ARE PREFERRED

Melt butter in medium skillet. Add in sugar, molasses, and water. Stir well. Add in apples, cover, and cook until tender. Remove cover and continue cooking until liquid is gone and apples are lightly browned.

Excellent served with sausage.

Serves 6 to 8

Johnny's Apple Chutney

2 CUPS APPLE CIDER VINEGAR
3/4 CUP BROWN SUGAR, PACKED
1 MEDIUM RED BELL PEPPER
2 LARGE JALAPENO PEPPERS, SEEDED AND CHOPPED
3 TBLSPS SWEET ONION, CHOPPED
4 TART, FIRM APPLES, PEELED, CORED, AND CHOPPED
  (TRANSPARENT, GRANNY SMITH, OR MCINTOSH WORK WELL)
1 TBLSP LEMON JUICE

In a large saucepan, bring the vinegar and sugar to a boil.
Stir until sugar is completely dissolved. Add in the bell
pepper, jalapenos, and onion and keep boiling for about
10 minutes. Remove from heat and stir in lemon juice.
Ladle into sterilized canning jars, seal, and process in
boiling water bath for 10 minutes. Serve with ham, sausage,
and egg dishes.

Makes 3 half-pint jars

Arkansas Applesauce

6 CUPS UNSWEETENED APPLE CIDER
5 POUNDS COOKING APPLES, CORED AND QUARTERED, (LIKE
   MCINTOSH, TRANSPARENT, JONATHANS, GRANNY SMITHS, OR ANY
   SWEET/TART VARIETY. YOU CAN COMBINE THEM, TOO.)
1/4 TSP SALT
1/2 TSP GROUND CINNAMON

In a large stockpot or canning kettle, bring the cider to
a boil. Continue boiling until reduced by half, about 8 to
10 minutes. Add in apples, salt, and cinnamon and bring
back to a boil. Reduce to simmer and continue cooking,
stirring occasionally for approximately 45 minutes.
Mixture should be thick. Run through a sieve and pour
into sterilized canning jars while hot. Process in a boiling
water bath. Can also be frozen.

Makes 3 quarts

Rath Bacon Strip Pancakes are the tender little hot cakes you make by pouring Aunt Jemima Pancake batter over cooked-crisp slices of our flavory Iowa bacon. Then bake as usual.

Complete recipe is on every Rath Black Hawk Bacon package.

Flapjacks, Pancakes, N' Waffles

A Little Know-How:

Pancakes, griddlecakes, hot cakes, or cake-cakes (as young kids call them) – they come in a vast rib-huggin' variety and need a few helpful hints to be put up right. If you use a no-stick griddle or pan, be aware that you won't get that grandma-effect of crispy, buttered edges. Try a butter-flavored spray on your skillet or griddle. Grandma often used a piece of bacon rind to sparingly slick up the cast iron griddle, but that's not necessary.

To test the griddle for the right heat, sprinkle a drop or two of water on the greased surface. If the water bounces around with enthusiasm, it's ready for the batter.

Do not let the griddle get too hot, especially not smoking hot. Pour on a puddle of batter about the size of a saucer, and flip it over when the top is covered in small bubbles. The second side takes only half the time. Cook until the right stage of golden brown. Use caution in attempting those griddle-hogging, Paul Bunyon-esque pancakes. They have a tendency to cook irregularly and are a major project to flip. Kids like the smaller 3-inch ones, especially those made from 3 circles to look like a famous mouse.

41

PANCAKES

Iowa Farm Boy's Corn 'Cakes

1/4 CUP SUGAR
2 TSPS BAKING POWDER
1 CUP FLOUR
1 TSP SALT
2 EGGS, WELL BEATEN
1 CUP MILK
1 CUP CORN (WHOLE KERNEL, FRESH OR CANNED)
1/3 CUP SHORTENING

In a medium bowl, combine sugar, baking powder, flour, and salt. Mix in the eggs and milk. Add in the corn and shortening and mix well. Pour on hot griddle in saucer-sized 'cakes and cook as directed on page 41. Serve hot.

Serves 2 to 3

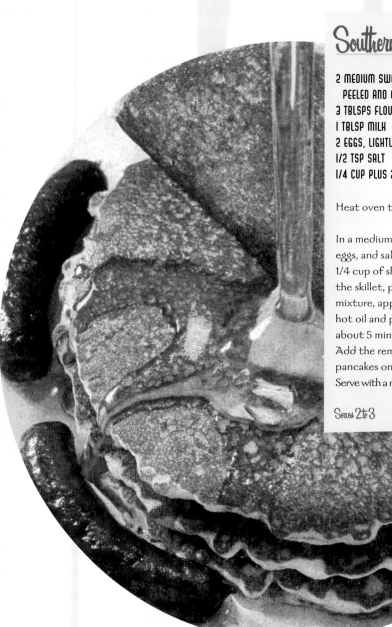

Southern Sweet Potato Pancakes

2 MEDIUM SWEET POTATOES (YAMS WILL WORK),
   PEELED AND GRATED
3 TBLSPS FLOUR
1 TBLSP MILK
2 EGGS, LIGHTLY BEATEN
1/2 TSP SALT
1/4 CUP PLUS 2 TBLSPS (6 TBLSPS) SHORTENING OR COOKING OIL

Heat oven to 300 degrees.

In a medium bowl, combine sweet potatoes, flour, milk, eggs, and salt. Take a nice cast iron skillet and heat the 1/4 cup of shortening or oil. According to the size of the skillet, place one or more portions of potato mixture, approximately 2 heaping tablespoons each, in hot oil and press flat with a spatula. Cook each pancake about 5 minutes on each side until brown and crispy. Add the remaining shortening as needed. Drain pancakes on paper towels and keep warm in oven. Serve with a nice selection of your favorite toppings.

Serves 2 to 3

Williamsburg Batter 'Cakes

3 CUPS CAKE FLOUR
2 TBLSPS BAKING POWDER
1 TSP SALT
3 EGG YOLKS, WELL BEATEN
1/4 CUP MAPLE SYRUP
1 1/8 CUPS MILK
1/4 CUP SHORTENING, MELTED

In a large bowl, combine the flour, baking powder, and salt. In a separate bowl, mix together the yolks, maple syrup, and milk; add to the dry ingredients and combine well. Let the shortening cool slightly, then add to the mixture and stir. Let batter stand for 30 minutes. To cook these traditionally, rub the griddle with a piece of salt pork before pouring on batter.

Serves 6 to 8

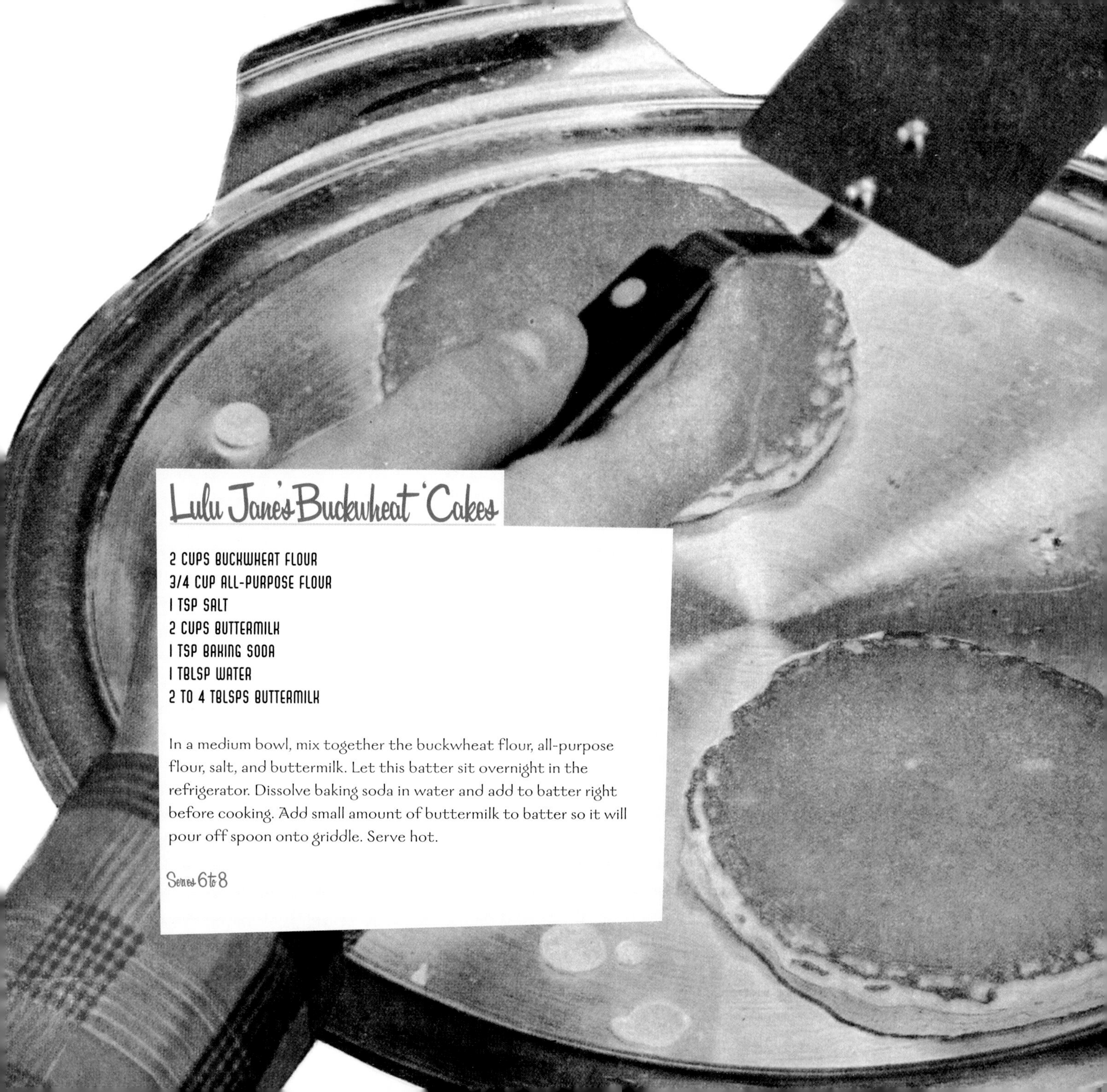

Lulu Jane's Buckwheat 'Cakes

2 CUPS BUCKWHEAT FLOUR
3/4 CUP ALL-PURPOSE FLOUR
1 TSP SALT
2 CUPS BUTTERMILK
1 TSP BAKING SODA
1 TBLSP WATER
2 TO 4 TBLSPS BUTTERMILK

In a medium bowl, mix together the buckwheat flour, all-purpose flour, salt, and buttermilk. Let this batter sit overnight in the refrigerator. Dissolve baking soda in water and add to batter right before cooking. Add small amount of buttermilk to batter so it will pour off spoon onto griddle. Serve hot.

Serves 6 to 8

Charity Breakfast Apple 'Cakes

1 1/4 CUPS ALL-PURPOSE FLOUR
1 1/4 CUPS YELLOW CORNMEAL
1/4 CUP SUGAR
1 1/2 TBLSPS BAKING POWDER
1/2 TSP GROUND CINNAMON
1/2 TSP SALT
2 EGGS, BEATEN
1 3/4 CUPS MILK
1/4 CUP + 2 TBLSPS CORN OR VEGETABLE OIL
2 SWEET/TART APPLES, PEELED, CORED, AND FINELY CHOPPED

In a medium bowl, combine flour, cornmeal, sugar, baking powder, cinnamon, and salt. In a separate bowl, beat the eggs and add the milk, oil, and apples. Stir egg and flour mixture together just until moistened. Cook on a greased griddle until underside is light brown. Turn carefully, as pancakes tend to fall apart easily. Serve with butter, maple syrup, and powdered sugar.

Serves 6 to 8

Mama Carol's Dutch Baby Pancakes

5 TBSP BUTTER
4 EGGS
1/2 TSP SALT
3/4 CUP FLOUR
3/4 CUP MILK

Preheat oven to 425 degrees and pull out two round glass pans.

Divide the butter into two chunks and place a chunk in each pan. Set pans in the oven while it preheats so the butter will melt. In a blender, combine the eggs, salt, flour, and milk. Blend until thoroughly mixed. Pour half of the batter into each pan and return them to the oven, placing them on the lowest shelf. Bake for 15 minutes and serve immediately with warm syrup, jam, or powered sugar and a lemon wedge.

Serves 2

Sunday Mornin' Hotcakes

2 CUPS ALL-PURPOSE FLOUR
1 CUP CORNMEAL
1 TSP SALT
1/2 TSP BAKING SODA
4 TSPS BAKING POWDER
1 CUP BRAN FLAKES
1 CUP WHOLE WHEAT FLOUR
2 EGGS, WELL BEATEN
4 CUPS BUTTERMILK

In a large bowl, combine the all-purpose flour, cornmeal, salt, baking soda, baking powder, bran flakes, and whole wheat flour. Add in the beaten eggs and buttermilk; mix well. Bake on ungreased griddle at medium heat, allowing 2 minutes per side.

Serves 6 to 8

Featherbed Farm's Pancakes

1 CUP WHOLE WHEAT PASTRY FLOUR
3/4 CUP ALL-PURPOSE FLOUR
1/4 CUP WHEAT GERM
1 1/2 TSP BAKING POWDER
1 TSP BAKING SODA
1/4 TSP SALT
2 CUPS MILK
3 TBLSPS BUTTER, MELTED
2 EGGS, BEATEN

In a large bowl, combine pastry flour, all-purpose flour, wheat germ, baking powder, baking soda, and salt. In a separate bowl, combine milk, butter, and eggs. Stir milk mixture into flour mixture until just moistened. Cook on a lightly greased griddle. Serve with butter and a selection of your favorite toppings.

Serves 4 to 6

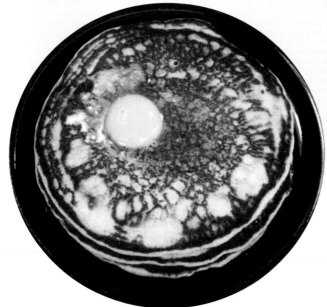

FLAPJACKS

These filling breakfast 'cakes get their name from the enormous logging camp cook shacks. Lumberjacks filed in at sunrise to stoke their robust appetites for a hard day's work in the woods. The camp cooks had a stockpile of flapjacks ready for the men to wolf down alongside platters of bacon, ham, eggs, and gallons of potent coffee.

Northwoods Flapjacks

2 CUPS ALL-PURPOSE FLOUR
2 TSPS BAKING POWDER
2 TBLSPS SUGAR
1/2 TSP SALT
4 EGGS, SEPARATED
2 TBLSPS BUTTER, MELTED
2 CUPS MILK

In a large bowl, combine flour, baking powder, sugar, and salt. Separately, beat the egg yolks, then the egg whites until fluffy. Beat together the butter, milk, and egg yolks with the flour mixture. Fold in the egg whites. Pour out into individual cakes and cook as directed on page 41.

Serves 4 to 6

Ritzville Washington's Wheat 'Cakes

Much of eastern Washington State is endless miles of rolling wheat fields. The sky appears enormous, the farmhouses like little islands of civilization, and the people old-time friendly.

2 CUPS MILK
2 EGG YOLKS, BEATEN
2 CUPS ALL-PURPOSE FLOUR
1 TBLSP SUGAR
1 TSP SALT
4 TBLSPS MELTED BUTTER (NOT SHORTENING!)
2 TSPS BAKING POWDER
2 EGG WHITES, BEATEN FLUFFY

In a large bowl, beat together the milk, egg yolks, flour, sugar, salt, butter, and baking powder. Beat into a smooth batter. Fold in egg whites. Cook on a lightly greased griddle.

Variations:

Substitute buttermilk for white milk and use baking soda in place of baking powder. Substitute 2 tablespoons sour cream for milk.

Serves 4 to 6

"It's too long since we've had those swell-tasting pancakes!"

Castlerock Blueberry Griddle 'Cakes

2 CUPS ALL-PURPOSE FLOUR
2 TSPS BAKING POWDER
1 TSP BAKING SODA
1 TSP SALT
3 TSPS SUGAR
1/4 CUP MELTED BUTTER
2 CUPS BUTTERMILK
2 EGGS, WELL BEATEN
1 CUP BLUEBERRIES, FRESH OR FROZEN

In a large bowl, combine flour, baking powder, baking soda, salt, sugar, melted butter, buttermilk, and eggs. Gently fold in blueberries. (If using frozen berries, thaw and drain first.) Cook on a lightly greased griddle.

Serves 4 to 6

Aebleskibers Danish Pancakes

2 CUPS ALL-PURPOSE FLOUR
1 TSP BAKING POWDER
1 TSP BAKING SODA
1/2 TSP SALT
2 TBLSPS SUGAR
2 CUPS BUTTERMILK
3 LARGE EGGS, SEPARATED
3 TBLSPS MELTED BUTTER

In a medium bowl, sift together the flour, baking powder, baking soda, salt, and sugar. In a small bowl, beat together the buttermilk and egg yolks. Add in butter. In a separate bowl, beat egg whites until stiff and fold into flour mixture. Cook as directed on page 41 using about 1/3 cup batter for each 'cake in a well greased pan.

*Nebraskans know that to make these pancakes authentically you must have an Aebleskiber pan: a small round cast iron frying pan.

Serves 4 to 6

Hannah's Healthnut Griddle 'Cakes

2/3 CUP WHOLE WHEAT FLOUR
3/4 CUP ALL-PURPOSE FLOUR
OR
1/2 CUP WHEAT GERM
1 CUP ALL-PURPOSE FLOUR

1 TBLSP SUGAR
1/2 TSP SALT
1 1/2 TSPS BAKING POWDER
1 EGG, WELL BEATEN
1 CUP MILK

In a medium bowl, combine all-purpose flour and whole wheat flour (or wheat germ) with sugar, salt, and baking powder. Combine egg and milk in a separate, small bowl then beat into dry ingredients. Continue beating until batter is smooth. Use about 1/4 cup for each griddle cake. Cook on a lightly greased griddle.

Serves 4 to 6

Vitex JUICER

NO SEEDS
NO PULP

EASY TO USE
EASY TO CLEAN

DESSERT PANCAKES

DESSERT PANCAKES
DESSERT PANCAKES

Cap'n Cook's Paradise Pancakes

3 CUPS OF YOUR FAVORITE BASIC BATTER
2 TBLSPS VEGETABLE OIL
1 TSP VANILLA
1 CUP PINEAPPLE JUICE, DIVIDED
1 TSP BAKING POWDER
1/4 POUND (1 CUBE) BUTTER, MELTED
1/2 CUP CRUSHED PINEAPPLE
1/4 CUP MACADAMIA NUTS, CHOPPED
1 CUP LIGHT KARO SYRUP

In a large bowl, blend well the batter with oil, vanilla, 1/2 cup juice, and baking powder. Keep mixture warm. In a separate, small saucepan, blend together the butter, second 1/2 cup juice, crushed pineapple, nuts, and syrup. Cook until just heated, stirring constantly. Cook pancakes as directed on page 41. Offer topping in bowl to spoon over these delectable 'cakes.

Serves 6 to 8

1840 French Dessert Pancakes

1/2 CUP ALL-PURPOSE FLOUR
1 EGG YOLK
1/8 TSP SALT
5 TBLSPS MILK
1 TBLSP BUTTER
1/4 CUP RASPBERRY JELLY OR YOUR FAVORITE
1/4 CUP POWDERED SUGAR

In a medium bowl, beat together flour, egg yolk, salt, and milk until smooth. If needed, add a little more milk to make batter the consistency of canned milk. Cover and chill batter for 30 minutes in refrigerator. Heat a heavy cast iron skillet and brush with butter (or use a non-stick spray). Pour in just enough batter to cover bottom of skillet, tipping skillet around as it cooks to make a thin pancake. Lightly brown on both sides and turn out on a plate. Spread pancake with jelly or jam and roll up. Sprinkle a little powdered sugar over the top. Keep warm.

Serves 4 to 6

Goldrush Sourdough Starter

6 TSPS DRY YEAST (2 PACKAGES)
1 3/4 CUPS WARM WATER (100 TO 110 DEGREES)
2 TBLSPS HONEY
2 CUPS ALL-PURPOSE FLOUR

Dissolve yeast in warm water. Mix in honey. In a large bowl, pour in yeast mixture and gradually add in flour, stirring until mixed thoroughly. Place in an earthenware jug or a half-gallon canning jar, or even a gallon mayonnaise jar will work. Store at room temperature for two days. Should be bubbly.

Ketchikan Kate's Sourdough Hotcakes

1 EGG, SEPARATED
1 TSP SALT
1 TSP BAKING SODA
1 TBLSP SUGAR
1 TBLSP OIL (CORN OIL OR CANOLA OIL)
1/2 CUP CANNED MILK, UNDILUTED
2 CUPS SOURDOUGH STARTER

In a medium bowl, beat well the egg yolk, salt, soda, sugar, oil, and canned milk. Beat egg white in a separate bowl until stiff but not dry. As quickly as possible, blend in the starter. Try not to break the bubbles as this is the leavening. Gently fold in the egg whites. Bake on a hot greased griddle.

To make waffles:
Use 2 eggs instead of 1 and use 1/4 cup of oil.

Serves 4 to 6

REAL NORTH WOODS FLAVOR

Like maple flavor? Then you'll *love* Log Cabin Syrup. It's got that rich, *real maple* taste . . . the result of a delicate, just-right blending of sugar and pure maple sugar syrups. One taste and you'll have visions of "sugarin' off time" in the North Woods! Get Log Cabin—in the familiar tin or handsome "antique" bottle—today.

Just made for each other — Log Cabin'n Waffles!

Buttermilk Cornmeal Waffles

1 CUP FLOUR
2 TSPS BAKING POWDER
1 TSP SUGAR
PINCH OF SALT
1 CUP YELLOW CORNMEAL
2 EGGS
2 CUPS BUTTERMILK
1/4 CUP MELTED BUTTER

Sift together flour, baking powder, sugar, and salt. Stir in cornmeal. In a small bowl, mix together eggs, buttermilk, and butter. Add to dry ingredients, stirring until just moistened. Cook in a hot waffle iron.

Serves 4 to 6

Country Supper Waffles

2 CUPS ALL-PURPOSE FLOUR
4 TSPS BAKING POWDER
1 TSP SALT
2 CUPS MILK
4 EGGS, SEPARATED
1 CUP MELTED BUTTER, MARGARINE, OR OIL

Plug in waffle iron. In a medium bowl, sift together flour, baking powder, and salt. In a separate bowl, combine egg yolks and milk until well blended. With your mixer, beat egg whites until stiff peaks form. Pour egg mixture into flour and beat just enough to moisten. Stir in slightly cooled butter. Fold in egg whites leaving little clumps of the white. Pour batter into a pitcher and pour enough batter onto waffle iron so it spreads to about 1 inch from edges. Close lid and do not open while waffle is baking. Bake until steaming stops or light on iron goes on. Loosen with fork and remove to warm platter. Reheat waffle iron before pouring on more batter. Serve with butter and your favorite syrups or fruit toppings.

Variations:
- Cook 6 slices of bacon. Drain on paper towels and crumble. Sprinkle into batter.
- Add 1/2 cup grated cheese to the batter.
- Sprinkle 2 tablespoons of your favorite chopped nuts over each waffle before baking.
- Add 1 cup well-drained whole kernel corn to the batter.
- Sprinkle 2 tablespoons chopped, cooked ham to each waffle before baking.

Serves 4 to 6

WAFFLES

Wheatland Waffles
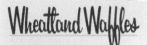

2 CUPS WHOLE WHEAT FLOUR
2 TSPS BAKING POWDER
3/4 TSP SALT
3 EGGS, SEPARATED
1 1/2 CUPS MILK
1/4 CUP MELTED SHORTENING

Preheat waffle iron. In a medium bowl, combine flour, baking powder, and salt. Stir well. In a separate bowl, beat the egg whites until fluffy. Beat the egg yolks and add in milk and shortening. Add all at once to the flour and blend until moistened. Fold in egg whites, leaving bits of white in batter. Pour onto preheated waffle iron and bake until steaming stops or light comes on. Serve hot with butter and your favorite toppings. Especially good with homemade apple butter. (See recipe on page 122.)

Serves 4 to 6

Rosewood Inn's Tender Waffles

3 EGGS, SEPARATED
2 CUPS FRESH BUTTERMILK
6 TBLSPS MELTED SHORTENING
2 CUPS ALL-PURPOSE FLOUR
1/2 TSP SALT
1 TBLSP BAKING POWDER
1 TSP SUGAR
1/2 TSP BAKING SODA
1 CUP COOKED WHITE RICE

Preheat waffle iron. In a medium bowl, beat egg yolks until thick
and yellow. Add in buttermilk and shortening and mix well. In a
separate bowl, sift together the flour, salt, baking powder, sugar,
and baking soda. Add to liquid mixture, and stir until smooth.
Add in rice and mix well. Beat egg whites until stiff and fold into
batter. Bake on hot waffle iron until it stops steaming or light
goes on. Serve with peach butter (see page 125).

Serves 4 to 6

FRENCH TOAST

FRENCH TOAST

FRENCH TOAST

Trudy's Baked French Toast

6 SLICES HOMEMADE WHITE BREAD OR FRENCH BREAD, THICK SLICED
2 EGGS
1 1/2 CUPS MILK
2 TSPS VANILLA
3 LARGE TART APPLES, PEELED, CORED, CUT INTO THIN SLICES
1/2 CUP SUGAR
1 TSP GROUND CINNAMON
1 1/2 TBLSPS BUTTER

Preheat oven to 400 degrees.

Lightly grease a 9 x 13 x 2-inch baking dish. Arrange bread in bottom of the dish. In a medium bowl, beat together the eggs, milk, and vanilla until smooth. Pour over the bread slices. Arrange the apple slices on top of bread. Combine sugar and cinnamon and sprinkle over the apple slices. Cut butter into small chunks and dot over all. Bake for 35 minutes or until apples are soft and custard is set. Serve with a variety of syrups, cream, or other toppings.

Serves 6

Rogue Valley Inn's French Toast

3 TSPS SUGAR
3/4 CUP MILK
3 LARGE EGGS
1 TSP VANILLA
3 TBLSPS BUTTER
12 SLICES WHITE OR FRENCH BREAD, THICK SLICED

In a shallow bowl, beat together the sugar, milk, eggs, and vanilla. Melt butter in a large, heavy skillet. When skillet is hot but not smoking, dip bread in egg mixture and place in pan. Brown 2 to 3 minutes on each side until golden brown. Keep cooked slices warm. Serve hot with an array of toppings such as powdered sugar, syrups (maple and fruit), honey, jams, etc. Some aficionados like cream cheese (soften it to room temperature first).

Serves 6

All-in-One
Casseroles 'N' One-Dish Meals

These dishes, some fitting the category of casseroles, are so easy and handy you'll be tempted to raise them above the status of morning essential. Add a nice salad fresh from your garden and plenty of warm, crusty bread, and you'll have a meal fit for any time. They also work well for when you have that troop of hungry kids, summertime company, or even a church potluck. Versatile is the word for these yummy one-dish wonders.

Cottage Casserole

The white sauce:

1 CUP COLD MILK
1 TBLSP ALL-PURPOSE FLOUR
1 TBLSP BUTTER

In a small skillet, melt the butter. Stir in flour until smooth and slightly nutty smelling. Over the lowest heat, slowly add in cold milk, stirring constantly until thickened.

The casserole:

1 CUP WHITE SAUCE (SEE ABOVE)
1 TBLSP FRESH PARSLEY, MINCED
3 MEDIUM COOKED POTATOES, SLICED
6 HARD-BOILED EGGS, SLICED
1 TSP SALT
1/2 TSP BLACK PEPPER
1/2 CUP SOFT BREADCRUMBS

Preheat oven to 375 degrees.

Grease a baking pan, 8 x 9 x 3-inch is good, but anything close will work. Alternate layers of potatoes and eggs. Sprinkle a little salt and pepper on each layer and pour the sauce over all. Spread crumbs over the top. Bake for 15 to 20 minutes.

Serves 4

Applegate River Breakfast Casserole

Linda lived on the picturesque Applegate River in southern Oregon for several years. This recipe came to her from a neighbor.

15 SLICES WHITE BREAD, THIN SLICED
6 TBLSPS (3/4 STICK) BUTTER
8 OUNCES LEAN BACON (TRY THE OLD-FASHIONED SLAB KIND WITH THE RIND REMOVED.)
6 EGGS
4 CUPS MILK
1/2 TSP SALT
1/4 TSP GROUND BLACK PEPPER
4 TO 6 OUNCES (ABOUT 1/2 CUP) SHARP CHEDDAR CHEESE
4 GREEN ONIONS (1/4 CUP), CHOPPED

Preheat oven to 350 degrees.

Spread one side of all slices of bread with butter. Sauté bacon in a medium skillet over medium heat until crisp. Drain on paper towels. Set aside. In a large bowl, beat together the eggs and milk until well blended. Mix in salt and pepper. Arrange bread in rows in a 8 x 13-inch baking dish, overlapping them. Crumble bacon. Sprinkle the cheese, onion, and bacon over the bread and pour the egg mixture over all. Let the dish sit overnight in the refrigerator or for at least 2 hours before baking. Bake approximately 50 minutes. Top should be puffed up above the baking dish edges, the center cooked through. Test with a toothpick or butter knife.

Serves 6 to 8

Fresh ideas

FOR BREAKFAST OR BRUNCH!

a Jolly Good way to start the day

Aunt Celia's Breakfast Strata

2 CUBES (1 CUP) BUTTER
10 OZ. CHEESE SPREAD (LIKE CHEEZ-WHIZ OR WISPRIDE), SOFTENED
16 SLICES BREAD, WHITE OR FRENCH WORK BEST
1 POUND PORK SAUSAGE, BROWNED AND DRAINED
2 - 8 OZ. CANS MUSHROOMS, SLICED
5 EGGS
2 CUPS WHOLE MILK
2 TSPS DIJON MUSTARD
1/4 TSP LEMON PEPPER

Preheat oven to 350 degrees.

In a small bowl, blend together the cheese spread and butter until smooth. Spread mixture on bread slices. In an 8 x 12-inch baking pan, place 8 slices face up. Layer over with the sausage and mushrooms. Top with the other 8 slices of bread, also face up. In a medium bowl, beat the eggs with milk and mustard and pour over the strata, sprinkle with lemon pepper and bake 30 minutes covered. Then bake another 30 minutes uncovered.

Serves 6 to 8

Beef Chips 'N' Taters

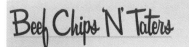

2 TBLSPS BUTTER
3 TBLSPS SWEET ONION, MINCED
1/4 POUND (6 OZ. JAR) DRIED CHIPPED BEEF
8 MEDIUM-SIZED POTATOES (ABOUT 2 POUNDS),
   WASHED, PEELED, SLICED THIN
2 TBLSPS ALL-PURPOSE FLOUR
1/4 TSP FRESHLY GROUND BLACK PEPPER
1 CUP SODA CRACKER CRUMBS

Preheat oven to 350 degrees.

In a small skillet, melt butter and sauté onions and chipped beef until onion is tender. Stir in flour. Add in milk, a little at a time, stirring constantly until mixture makes a smooth, thick sauce. Place a thick layer of potatoes in a large greased baking dish, about 12 x 13 x 3 inches. Sprinkle with a little pepper and pour over some of the sauce mixture. Continue layering and top with the cracker crumbs. Bake for 1 hour.

Serves 6

Homesteader Scrapple

2 CUPS YELLOW CORNMEAL
3 TSPS SALT
8 CUPS WATER, DIVIDED
1 1/2 TO 2 CUPS COOKED PORK OR HAM, CHOPPED
3 TBLSPS SHORTENING

In a medium bowl, stir well the cornmeal, salt, and 2 cups water. Get all the lumps out. Meanwhile, put a 6 to 8-quart kettle on high heat and bring the 6 cups of water to a boil. Slowly stir the cornmeal mixture into the boiling water. Stir constantly with a long-handled wooden spoon or mixing spoon, as the cornmeal has a tendency to blurp up and burn the cook. Cook at least 10 minutes. Stir in pork. Pour into greased loaf pans and cool overnight in refrigerator. In the morning, slice 1/2-inch thick. Heat shortening in a heavy skillet and fry slices until golden brown on both sides and the edges are crispy. If desired, serve with honey, syrup, apple butter, or applesauce.

Serves 6 to 8

Red Flannel Jammies Hash

3 CUPS LEAN GROUND ROUND
3 LARGE POTATOES, COOKED AND CHOPPED
1 SMALL ONION, CHOPPED
4 MEDIUM BEETS, COOKED AND MINCED
1/2 TSP COARSELY GROUND BLACK PEPPER
1 TSP SALT
1 TBLSP BUTTER
4 SLICES LEAN BACON
1/2 CUP CREAM

Preheat oven to 350 degrees.

In a large mixing bowl, combine the ground beef, potatoes, onion, beets, pepper, salt, and butter. Press into a 9-inch square baking dish, top with bacon, and pour cream over all. Bake for 40 minutes. Bacon should be crisp. Cut into squares to serve.

Serves 6

My Pal's Simple Egg Dish

This is a favorite with kids and is also terrific for camping.

1/2 POUND GOOD QUALITY LEAN BACON, THICK-SLICED
1 CAN (15 1/4 OZ.) WHOLE KERNEL CORN
6 LARGE EGGS, BEATEN

In a large heavy skillet, fry the bacon over medium heat until crispy and browned. Remove from heat. Drain on paper towels and cut into 1-inch sections. Drain off all but about 2 tablespoons of the bacon grease and return skillet to heat. Drain corn and pour into skillet. Cook, stirring often, for about 2 minutes. Add back in the bacon and mix with corn. Pour in beaten eggs and cook as you would for scrambled eggs, making sure not to let the eggs get too dry. Serve hot with homemade biscuits.

Serves 4

Hearty Man's Quiche

UNBAKED 9-INCH PIE CRUST
8 OZ. PORK SAUSAGE
4 HARD-BOILED EGGS, CHOPPED
1 CUP (4 OZ.) SWISS CHEESE, SHREDDED
1 CUP (4 OZ.) CHEDDAR CHEESE, SHREDDED
3 EGGS, BEATEN
1 1/2 CUPS CREAM OR HALF AND HALF
1/2 TSP SALT
1/8 TSP COARSELY GROUND BLACK PEPPER

Preheat oven to 350 degrees.

Bake pie shell for 7 minutes. In a medium skillet, fry sausage until browned. Drain well. Spread the hard-boiled eggs in bottom of pie shell. Top with sausage, Swiss, and cheddar cheese. In a small bowl, combine eggs, cream, salt, and pepper. Pour over cheese mixture. Bake for 30 to 35 minutes or until set like a custard. Let stand 5 minutes before serving.

Serves 6

1849 Hangtown Fry

1 DOZEN SMALL OYSTERS
1/4 CUP ALL-PURPOSE FLOUR
1/2 TSP SALT
1/8 TSP COARSELY GROUND BLACK PEPPER
1 EGG, WELL BEATEN
1/2 CUP FINE CRACKER CRUMBS
4 TBLSPS BUTTER
8 EGGS

Drain oysters and pat dry with paper towels. Heat
butter in heavy skillet. In a small bowl, combine flour
with salt and pepper. Dip each oyster in the flour
mixture, then in the beaten egg, then in cracker
crumbs, and fry in butter. Cook until nicely browned
on both sides (it only takes a few minutes). Beat
together the 8 eggs and pour over cooked oysters in
skillet. Cook until firm, turn with a large spatula, and
cook second side only a minute or two. Serve with
sourdough bread or cornbread.

Serves 4

Blue Ridge Cornmeal Loaf

1 CUP YELLOW CORNMEAL
1 CUP MILK
2 CUPS BOILING WATER
1 TSP SALT
1/2 POUND (1 CUP) SHARP CHEDDAR CHEESE, CUBED
1/2 CUP SHORTENING
1/2 CUP ALL-PURPOSE FLOUR

In a medium saucepan, stir together cornmeal and
milk. Add boiling water and cook over medium heat,
stirring constantly until mixture has thickened, about
5 minutes. Reduce to low heat, cover, and simmer for
another 10 minutes, stirring occasionally. Remove from
heat and add in salt and cheese. Continue stirring
until cheese melts. Spoon into a loaf pan and let cool;
overnight is best. When cool and solid, turn out onto
a plate and slice 1/2-inch thick. Heat shortening in a
heavy skillet. Dip slices in flour and fry until crispy and
golden brown on both sides. Serve with bacon, ham,
or sausages. Offer butter and syrup.

Serves 4 to 6

Finger-Lickin' Biscuits N'Breads
Tender and Fluffy Oven Delights

Breakfast is definitely not breakfast without a plateful of hot homemade biscuits, cornbread, scones, or other butter-able breads. Linda's grandmother made the absolute best biscuits on this planet, and Linda's still trying to duplicate her recipe. She also served up yummy spoon bread, dripping in butter and maple syrup, and as close to sinfully good as a body can get. Choose the traditional favorites to match your tastes or consider sampling classics from someone else's kitchen.

Gramma Griffin's Famous Biscuits

4 CUPS ALL-PURPOSE FLOUR
2 TSP SALT
2 TBLSPS BAKING POWDER
2/3 CUP SHORTENING
1 1/2 CUPS MILK

Heat oven to 425 degrees.

In a large bowl, combine flour, salt, and baking powder. Cut in shortening by crumbling with your fingers (or use a pastry blender). The dough should be crumbly. With a fork, add in the milk until mixture sticks together and forms a ball. Move dough to a lightly floured board or other surface. Knead gently 8 to 10 times and roll to 1/2-inch thickness. Cut with floured, 2-inch round cutter and place on ungreased baking sheet. Bake for 12 to 14 minutes or until light golden brown.

Makes about 24 biscuits.

Variations:

Drop Biscuits: Prepare as instructed only increase milk to 2 cups. Do not knead or roll out. Drop from tablespoon onto ungreased baking sheet.

Buttermilk Biscuits: Prepare as instructed only add 1/4 tsp baking soda to dry ingredients and substitute buttermilk for the white milk.

Whole Wheat Biscuits: Prepare as instructed only substitute 1 cup of the all-purpose flour with whole wheat. Roll the biscuits to 5/8-inch thickness and cut.

Sadie's Soda Biscuits

2 CUPS ALL-PURPOSE FLOUR
1 TSP BAKING SODA
1 TSP CREAM OF TARTAR
1/8 TSPS SALT
4 TBLSP SHORTENING
1 CUP BUTTERMILK

Preheat oven to 450 degrees.

In a medium bowl, combine flour, soda, cream of tartar, and salt. Add in shortening and mix together with your fingers or a pastry cutter until mixture is crumbly. Using a fork, stir in the buttermilk until a soft dough is formed. On a lightly floured board, roll the dough until 1/2-inch thick and cut with a biscuit cutter. Bake for 10 to 12 minutes or until lightly browned. Serve hot with butter, jam, jelly, honey, or homestyle gravy.

Makes 12 biscuits

Grandma Bowden's Famous Biscuits

2 CUPS ALL-PURPOSE FLOUR
1/2 TSP SALT
4 TSPS BAKING POWDER
1/2 TSP CREAM OF TARTAR
2 TSPS SUGAR
1/2 CUP SHORTENING
2/3 CUP PLUS 2 TBSP MILK

Preheat oven to 450 degrees.

Sift together flour, salt, baking powder, cream of tartar, and sugar. Cut in the shortening until it resembles corse cornmeal (crumbly). Add in the milk and mix very lightly with a fork. Dough should be moist and slightly sticky. Turn out onto a floured board and knead several times. Roll it out to 1/2-inch thickness and cut out 2-inch circles. Bake for 10 minutes or until brown.

Makes about 12 biscuits

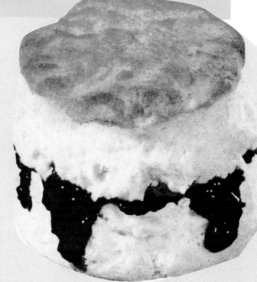

Cripple Creek Crispy Biscuits

2 CUPS ALL-PURPOSE FLOUR
4 TSPS BAKING POWDER
3/4 TSP SALT
6 TBLSPS BUTTER OR SHORTENING
3/4 CUP MILK

Preheat oven to 425 degrees.

In a medium bowl, sift together flour, baking powder, and salt. Cut in the butter with a pastry knife or your fingers until mixture is crumbly. Moisten with milk and mix until a soft dough forms. Turn out on floured board, fold over twice, and roll out to thin 1/2-inch. Cut into small rounds, about 2 inches, and bake for 12 to 15 minutes. Watch carefully, as they burn easily. These must be served hot. Offer butter, honey, jam, or jelly of your choice.

Serves 4

Powder River Valley Breakfast Biscuits

2 CUPS ALL-PURPOSE FLOUR
1 TBLSP BAKING POWDER
2 TSPS SUGAR
1 TSP SALT
1/4 CUP SHARP CHEDDAR CHEESE, FINELY GRATED
1/4 CUP COOKED HAM, MINCED
2 TBLSPS GREEN ONIONS OR SCALLIONS, MINCED
3/4 CUP HEAVY CREAM
3 TBLSPS BUTTER, SOFTENED

Preheat oven to 375 degrees.

In a large bowl, sift together the flour, baking powder, sugar, and salt. Add in the cheese, ham, onions, and cream, and mix gently until it forms a soft dough. Turn the dough onto a floured board and knead for 1 or 2 minutes, just until it sticks together. Do not over knead, as it will make dough tough. Pat dough out into 1-inch thickness. Use a 2-inch biscuit cutter or water glass, and cut into 12 biscuits. Brush each biscuit with softened butter and bake on ungreased baking sheet for 18 to 20 minutes or until golden brown. Serve hot with your favorite mouth-watering topping.

Makes 12 biscuits

Southern Exposure Sweet Potato Biscuits

2 CUPS ALL-PURPOSE FLOUR
4 TSPS BAKING POWDER
1 TSP SALT
2/3 CUP SHORTENING (THE OLD TIME RECIPE CALLS FOR LARD, BUT....)
1 CUP COOKED SWEET POTATOES, PEELED AND MASHED
1/4 CUP MILK (APPROXIMATELY)

Preheat oven to 400 degrees.

In a large bowl, sift together the flour, baking powder, and salt.
Blend in the shortening with a pastry cutter or your fingers.
Stir in sweet potatoes. Add in enough milk to make dough
soft. Turn out on floured board and knead only a minute or
two. Roll to 1/2-inch thick and cut with floured, 2-inch biscuit
cutter. Place on ungreased baking sheet for 20 minutes or until
golden brown. Serve with butter, honey, jam, or other favorite
topping.

Makes about 15 biscuits

Maisie's Cheese Biscuits

3 CUPS ALL-PURPOSE FLOUR
1 TBLSP + 1 1/2 TSPS BAKING POWDER
1 TBLSP SUGAR
2 TSP SALT
3/4 CUP SHARP CHEDDAR CHEESE
2 1/2 CUPS HEAVY CREAM
3 TBLSPS BUTTER, SOFTENED

Preheat oven to 350 degrees.

In a large bowl, sift together the flour, baking powder, sugar, and salt. Add in the cheese and cream, and blend together until it forms a soft dough. Turn out onto a floured board and knead 6 to 8 times. Using a lightly floured rolling pin, roll out to 1/2-inch thickness. Using a 2-inch biscuit cutter or water glass, cut into about 12 biscuits. Mold together remaining scraps to make more. Brush each biscuit with softened butter and bake on cookie sheet for 18 to 20 minutes or until light golden brown.
**If you are not a "chees-a-holic," you may want to reduce the amount of grated cheese to 1/2 cup.

Makes about 12 biscuits

Fall Favorite Pumpkin Biscuits

2 CUPS ALL-PURPOSE FLOUR
3 TBLSPS SUGAR
4 TSPS BAKING POWDER
1/2 TSP SALT
1/2 TSP CINNAMON
1/2 CUP BUTTER
1/3 CUP PECANS, CHOPPED (YOU CAN SUBSTITUTE WALNUTS OR ALMONDS)
1/2 CUP HALF AND HALF
2/3 CUP CANNED PUMPKIN

Preheat oven to 425 degrees.

In a large bowl, sift together the flour, sugar, baking powder, salt, and cinnamon. Cut in the butter with a pastry knife or with your fingers until mixture is crumbly. Stir in pecans. Combine half and half and pumpkin and stir into the flour mixture. Dough will be a little stiff. Turn out onto a floured board and knead 4 or 5 times. Roll out to 1/2-inch thickness and cut with a 2-inch biscuit cutter. Place on greased baking sheet and bake about 20 minutes. Watch carefully so they don't burn. They should be light golden brown. Serve with butter and honey.

Makes about 20 biscuits

Off-the-Wagon Rolls

1 PACKAGE (3 OZ.) DRY YEAST
1/4 CUP WARM WATER (100 TO 110 DEGREES)
2 TBLSPS SUGAR
1 EGG, SLIGHTLY BEATEN
2/3 CUP MILK
1 TSP SALT
2 TBLSPS SHORTENING, MELTED
4 1/2 CUPS ALL-PURPOSE FLOUR
1/4 CUP + 2 TBLSPS BEER

In a large bowl, dissolve yeast in warm water. Add in sugar, egg, milk, salt, and shortening. Mix well. Gradually beat in flour, alternating with a few tablespoons of beer, until you have a dough just dry enough to knead. Turn out on floured board and knead until bubbles appear in dough, about 6 to 8 minutes. Butter dough, turn over in a large bowl, and butter top. Cover with clean cloth and let rise for 1 1/2 hours in a warm place (80 degrees is ideal). Roll out dough and form into rolls with your hands. Place on baking sheet and let rise again for another 1 1/2 hours. Preheat oven to 475 degrees. Bake until rolls are light brown. Watch closely as they bake quickly (8 to 10 minutes).

Makes about 30 Parkerhouse-style rolls

Easy-Does-It Rolls

2 CUPS SELF-RISING FLOUR
1/4 CUP MAYONNAISE, THE REGULAR KIND, NOT LIGHT OR FAT-FREE
1 CUP WHOLE MILK

Heat oven to 425 degrees.

Grease a twelve-cup muffin tin. The sections should be about 2 1/2-inch size. In a medium bowl, combine the flour, mayonnaise, and milk. Stir only enough to moisten flour (use a fork). Divide dough equally between muffin cups. Bake for 20 minutes. Serve warm with butter, honey, or jam.

Makes 12 Rolls

HOMEMADE Hot Rolls!

Heart 'N' Soul Biscuits 'N' Gravy

This is a true farmland standby, often found in those tiny hole-in-the-wall cafes where the locals come by at sunrise. They share the latest corn prices, discuss the new 'Deere cousin George bought, drink strong coffee with real cream, and fill up for the long day's work on scrumptious biscuits n' gravy. (It is never biscuits and gravy!)

The biscuits:
1 3/4 CUPS ALL-PURPOSE FLOUR
2 TSPS BAKING POWDER
1 TSP SALT
4 TBLSPS (1/4 CUP OR 1/2 STICK) BUTTER
1/3 CUP PLAIN YOGURT
1/2 CUP + 2 TBLSPS MILK

The sausage:
1 1/2 POUNDS PORK SAUSAGE (UNSEASONED)
1 TBLSP FRESH SAGE, MINCED, OR 1 TSP DRIED
3/4 TSP SALT
1/4 TSP FRESHLY GROUND BLACK PEPPER
1/2 TSP PAPRIKA

The gravy:
3 TBLSPS BUTTER
3 TBLSPS ALL-PURPOSE FLOUR
2 1/4 CUPS MILK
1/2 TSP SALT
1/4 TSP FRESHLY GROUND BLACK PEPPER

To make the biscuits:

Preheat oven to 425 degrees. In a large bowl, sift together the flour, baking powder, and salt. Using a pastry knife or your fingers, blend in the butter until mixture is crumbly. Using a fork, mix in the yogurt and milk until the dough is sticky. Turn onto a floured board and knead only a minute or two. Roll it out to 1/2-inch thick and cut into biscuits with a 2-inch biscuit or cookie cutter or a small water glass. Bake 18 to 20 minutes until biscuits are puffy and lightly browned.

Makes 10 biscuits.

The sausages:

While the biscuits are baking, place the sausage, sage, salt, pepper, and paprika in a large bowl and mix well. Shape into 8 small patties and fry in a heavy skillet over medium-high heat. Patties should be brown inside and out, about 8 minutes on each side. Remove from skillet and keep warm.

To make the gravy:

Take the same skillet you browned the sausages in and add enough butter to cover the bottom. Place over medium-high heat and scrape the pan to loosen the bits on the bottom of the skillet. Reduce heat to medium and slowly add in flour, stirring constantly until it has soaked up the butter mixture. Keep stirring until flour mixture is golden brown. Slowly add in milk, stirring constantly, until gravy thickens to about the consistency of thick cream. Season with salt and pepper.

To serve:

Divide two biscuits in half and place on a plate. Top with two sausage patties followed by the gravy.

Serves 4 to 6

Indiana Spoonbread

This is a fluffier spoon bread than the Sunday Mornin' Spoonbread.

1 CUP YELLOW CORNMEAL
1 1/2 CUPS BOILING WATER
2 TBLSPS BUTTER, SOFTENED
3 EGGS, SEPARATED
1 CUP BUTTERMILK
1 TSP SUGAR
1 TSP SALT
1 TSP BAKING POWDER
3/4 TSP BAKING SODA

Preheat oven to 375 degrees.

In a large bowl, pour in the cornmeal and stir in boiling water. Continue to stir until mixture cools. Add in butter, egg yolks, and mix well. Stir in buttermilk, sugar, salt, baking powder, and baking soda. With your electric mixer, beat the egg whites until soft peaks form. Fold beaten whites into the cornmeal mixture and pour batter into a greased, 2-quart casserole or baking dish. Bake 45 to 50 minutes. Spoon bread should be puffy and set in the center. Serve immediately, as it has a tendency to fall. Serve with butter.

Serves 8

Sunday Mornin' Spoonbread

1 1/2 CUPS MILK
1 CUP YELLOW OR WHITE CORNMEAL
1 1/2 CUPS FRESH CORN OFF THE COB (ABOUT 2 EARS)
1 TSP SALT
4 LARGE EGGS, SEPARATED
1/2 TSP BAKING POWDER

Preheat oven to 375 degrees.

In a large saucepan, bring the milk to a simmer over medium heat. Add in the cornmeal, fresh corn, and salt, and cook for about 5 minutes. Mixture should be the consistency of mush. Stir often, then cool. In a medium bowl, lightly beat the egg yolks. Add in the cornmeal mixture and baking powder. Blend well. In a large bowl, beat the egg whites until they form soft peaks. Fold in the cornmeal mixture. Pour into a buttered 2-quart casserole dish and bake for 35 to 40 minutes or until center is set. Test for doneness by poking a butter knife in center. When it comes out clean, the spoonbread is done.

Serves 6 to 8

Monterey Bay Chile Cornbread

1 1/4 CUPS YELLOW OR WHITE CORNMEAL
1 CUP ALL-PURPOSE FLOUR
3 TBLSPS SUGAR
1 TBLSP BAKING POWDER
1 TSP SALT
2 LARGE EGGS
1 1/4 CUPS MILK
6 TBLSPS BUTTER
1/2 CUP SWEET ONION, FINELY CHOPPED
1/4 TO 1/2 CUP CANNED GREEN CHILIES (ADJUST TO YOUR TASTE
   AND TRY OTHER VARIETIES)
2 TBLSPS CHILE POWDER

Preheat oven to 425 degrees.

In a large bowl, combine the cornmeal, flour, sugar,
baking powder, and salt. In a separate bowl, beat eggs
with the milk. Add in the cornmeal mixture and stir
just until mixture is no longer lumpy. In a small skillet,
melt the butter and cook onion over medium heat
until tender. Remove from heat, stir in green chilies
and chile powder, and add to cornmeal mixture. Pour
into a greased 9-inch square baking pan and bake for
20 to 25 minutes. Cornbread should be firm in center.
Test with a toothpick or butter knife.

Serves 6 to 8

Aunt Ida's Yeast Cornbread

1 CUP WATER
1 CUP YELLOW CORNMEAL
3 TSPS SALT, DIVIDED
1 PACKAGE (2 1/4 TSPS) DRY YEAST
1/2 CUP WARM WATER (100 TO 110 DEGREES)
1 TBLSP SUGAR
1 CUP WARM MILK
1/4 CUP LIGHT BROWN SUGAR
4 CUPS ALL-PURPOSE FLOUR

Preheat oven to 425 degrees.

In a small saucepan, bring the water to a boil over
high heat. Use a whisk to blend in the cornmeal, a
little at a time, with 1 teaspoon salt. Reduce to
low and cook for about 1 minute. Mixture should
be the consistency of mush. Let cool. In a small
bowl, sprinkle yeast over warm water, stir in, and
let stand about 10 minutes. Mixture should
bubble. Add yeast to cornmeal mixture, and mix
in the milk, remaining 2 teaspoons salt, and brown
sugar. Add flour a cup at a time until the dough
becomes smooth. This is easiest with a mixer and
dough hook. Turn onto a floured board, and
knead 3 to 4 times. Place dough in a large, greased
bowl and let sit for about 2 hours in a warm
place. Butter two 9 x 5-inch bread pans. Divide
dough, form into loaves, press into bread pans,
and let sit for about 45 minutes or until about
double in size. Bake for 10 minutes, then reduce
heat to 350 and bake another 20 to 25 minutes
or until loaves are lightly brown. Turn out of pans
and cool on wire racks to room temperature
before slicing. Serve with all of the yummy jams,
jellies, honey, and other favorite toppings.

Makes 2 loaves

Smoky Mountain Corn Pone

1 CUP SUGAR
1/2 CUP BUTTER OR BUTTER-FLAVORED SHORTENING
2 EGGS
1 1/2 CUPS CORNMEAL
1 1/2 CUPS ALL-PURPOSE FLOUR
3 TSPS BAKING POWDER
1/2 TSP SALT
1 1/2 CUPS MILK

Preheat oven to 350 degrees.

In a medium bowl, cream together sugar and shortening. Add eggs one at a time and beat mixture well. In a separate bowl, combine cornmeal, flour, baking powder, and salt. Add to the creamed mixture alternately with the milk. Pour into a greased and floured 9 x 13-inch baking pan. Bake for 45 minutes.

Serves 4 to 6

Hole 'N' Hearty Bran Muffins

1 CUP RED BRAN
1/2 CUP WHOLE WHEAT FLOUR
1/2 CUP WHEAT GERM
1/2 CUP SUNFLOWER SEEDS (OPTIONAL)
1 CUP RAISINS
3 TSPS BAKING POWDER
1 EGG, WELL BEATEN
1 CUP MILK
1/3 CUP VEGETABLE OIL (CANOLA IS ALSO GOOD)
3 TBLSPS DARK MOLASSES
1 TSP VANILLA

Preheat oven to 350 degrees.

In a large bowl, combine bran, flour, wheat germ, sunflower seeds, raisins, and baking powder. In a separate bowl, mix together the egg, milk, oil, molasses, and vanilla. Pour liquid mixture slowly into dry ingredients, and mix only until moist. Grease a 12-section muffin tin (or use papers) and fill each section about 3/4 full. Bake for 20 minutes.

Makes 12

Heritage Scones

3 EGGS
2 CUPS MILK
3/4 CUP VEGETABLE OIL
6 CUPS ALL-PURPOSE FLOUR
3 TBLSPS BAKING POWDER

Preheat oven to 450 to 475 degrees.

In a small bowl, beat together eggs, milk, and oil. In a separate large bowl, sift together flour and baking powder. Mix together egg mixture with flour to form a soft dough. Turn out on a floured board and pat out to about 1/2-inch thick. Do not knead. Cut into triangles and place close together on a baking sheet. Bake for 5 to 10 minutes, only until scones are light brown. Serve with yummy homemade jam, honey, and, of course, butter.

Variations:
- To use as shortcake, add 4 tablespoons sugar.
- Add 1 cup grated cheese.
- Add 1 cup raisins, chopped dates, or other dried fruit.

Makes about 2 dozen

it's a Sweetheart of a breakfast!

Happy Monkey Bread

1/4 CUP BUTTER
1/2 CUP SUGAR
1 EGG
1 TSP VANILLA
1/2 TSP SALT
1/2 TSP BAKING SODA
1 1/2 CUPS BANANAS, MASHED
1 1/2 CUPS ALL-PURPOSE FLOUR
1 CUP BRAN
3/4 CUP WALNUTS, FINELY CHOPPED
2 TSPS BAKING POWDER

Preheat oven to 350 degrees.

In a medium bowl, cream together the butter, sugar, and egg, then add in vanilla. In a separate bowl, mix together the water, salt, and soda with the bananas. Combine the flour, bran, walnuts, and baking powder, and fold into the banana mixture. The dough should be stiff. Pour into a loaf pan and bake for 50 minutes or until toothpick inserted in center comes out clean.

Makes 1 loaf

Basic White Bread

1 PACKAGE DRY YEAST (2 1/4 TSPS)
2 1/2 CUPS WARM WATER (100 TO 110 DEGREES), DIVIDED
3 TBSPS SUGAR
2 TSPS SALT
2 1/2 TBLSPS SHORTENING, MELTED
6 TO 7 CUPS FLOUR

In a small bowl or measuring cup, dissolve yeast in 1/2 cup warm water. In a large mixing bowl, combine together the sugar, salt, remaining 2 cups warm water, and shortening. Add in yeast mixture. Then add the flour a little at a time until mixture forms a soft dough. Turn out onto a floured board and knead until dough becomes shiny smooth, about 10 minutes. Place in a greased bowl, cover, and let rise in a warm spot until double in size, about 2 hours. Punch down. Divide in half, form into loaves, and place in greased bread pans. Poke a few holes in the top of each with a fork and let rise again, about 2 hours. Preheat oven to 375 degrees. Bake for 25 to 30 minutes until tops are golden brown. Cool for 10 minutes. Remove loaves and place on wire rack.

Makes 2 loaves

NO SCORCHING! NO BURNING! NO WATCHING!

saucy-melter ™ Reg.

Fits on any pot you're using. The steam melts the sauce in a jiffy ...or use over a low flame, if desired

Basic Wheat Bread

2 PACKAGES DRY YEAST (4 1/2 TSPS)
4 CUPS WARM WATER (100 TO 110 DEGREES)
1/2 CUP BUTTER OR MARGARINE, SOFTENED
1/4 CUP DARK MOLASSES
1/2 CUP HONEY
1 1/2 TSP SALT
6 CUPS WHOLE WHEAT FLOUR
4 CUPS WHITE FLOUR

Dissolve yeast in warm water. In a large bowl, combine butter, molasses, honey, and salt. Mix together well. Add in yeast mixture. Mix in both of the flours a little at a time. Turn onto floured board and knead until smooth and shiny, about 10 minutes. Put in a greased bowl in a warm place, and let rise until double its size. Punch down. Let dough rest about 10 minutes. Shape into 4 loaves and place in greased bread pans. Let rise again about 1 hour. Preheat oven to 375 degrees and bake for 35 to 40 minutes.

Makes 4 loaves

Poppy's Home Cornbread

1 CUP ALL-PURPOSE FLOUR
3 TSPS BAKING POWDER
1 TSP SALT
3 TBLSPS SUGAR
1 CUP CORNMEAL
2 EGGS, SLIGHTLY BEATEN
1 CUP MILK
1/4 CUP SHORTENING, MELTED

Preheat oven to 400 degrees.

In a medium bowl, sift together the flour, baking powder, salt, sugar, and cornmeal. In a separate bowl, beat together eggs, milk, and melted shortening, and add to flour mixture. Mix only long enough to moisten. Pour into a greased 8 x 8 x 2-inch baking pan and bake for 30 minutes. Serve hot out of the oven with butter, honey, jam, or jelly.

Makes 6 to 8 servings

Old English Wheat Bread

2 CUPS MILK, SCALDED
2 TBLSPS BUTTER, DIVIDED
2 TSP SALT
1/2 CUP SUGAR
1 PACKAGE (2 1/4 TSPS) DRY YEAST
1/2 CUP WARM WATER (100 TO 110 DEGREES)
POTATO WATER (LEFTOVER FROM BOILING POTATOES)
2 CUPS ALL-PURPOSE FLOUR
2 CUPS WHOLE WHEAT FLOUR
1 TBLSP BUTTER

After scalding milk in saucepan, stir in 1 tablespoon butter, salt, and sugar. Cool to lukewarm and pour into a large bowl. Dissolve yeast in warm potato water. Stir into milk mixture. Add in all-purpose white flour and beat until smooth. Let rise in a warm place until bubbly. Add in whole wheat flour a little at a time, beating well. Butter or grease 2 bread pans. Divide dough and form into loaves. Place in pans and butter tops. Let rise until double in size. Preheat oven to 375 degrees and bake bread for 40 minutes.

Makes 2 loafs

Pigeon Hollow Farm's Oatmeal Bread

1 CUP ROLLED OATS
2 CUPS MILK, SCALDED
1 PACKAGE (2 1/4 TSPS) DRY YEAST
1/2 CUP WARM WATER (100 TO 110 DEGREES)
1/2 CUP MOLASSES
1 TSP SALT
1 TBLSP BUTTER, MELTED
4 1/2 CUPS ALL-PURPOSE FLOUR

In a large bowl, pour in oats and cover with the hot milk. Let stand until lukewarm. Dissolve yeast in warm water and add to oat mixture. Add molasses, salt, and butter. Mix well. Add half the flour and beat until smooth. Add remaining flour and mix well. Cover with a clean kitchen towel and set in a warm place to rise until double in size. Form into 2 loaves and place in greased 9 x 5 x 2-inch loaf pans. Let rise again until double in size. Preheat oven to 425 degrees and bake for 15 minutes. Turn down heat to 350 degrees and bake for another 35 minutes or until done. Remove from pans at once and cool on wire rack. Serve with butter, your favorite jam, jelly, or honey.

Makes 2 loafs

Sweeties

Appalachian Apple Fritters

1 CUP ALL-PURPOSE FLOUR
1 1/2 TSP BAKING POWDER
1/2 TSP SALT
2 TBLSPS SUGAR
1 EGG
1/2 CUP PLUS 1 TBLSP WHOLE MILK
1 1/2 CUPS APPLES, PARED AND DICED
  (CHOOSE A SWEET/TART VARIETY LIKE MCINTOSH)
COOKING OIL

In a medium bowl, sift together the flour, baking powder, salt, and sugar. In a separate bowl, beat together the eggs and milk. Pour into the flour mixture and beat until smooth. Stir apples into the batter. Heat oil in a heavy skillet. Drop batter into hot oil and fry until golden brown, turning once, about 2 minutes per side. Drain well on paper towels and serve warm.

Makes 12 fritters

Golden Valley Dumplings

In many Amish kitchens, these dumplings are served for breakfast. In other homes, they appear only as dessert, traditionally with home-canned peaches and heavy cream.

Using your favorite white bread dough (see page 88 for a suggested recipe), pull off bun-sized balls (about 3-inches in diameter), and place in a 2-inch deep, buttered baking dish or the top section of a rice steamer. Steam over boiling water for 30 minutes. Serve hot with fruit and milk or half and half.

Serves 6 to 8

Harvest Time Potato Doughnuts

1 PACKAGE DRY YEAST (2 1/4 TSPS)
1/4 CUP WARM WATER (100 TO 110 DEGREES)
1/4 CUP SHORTENING
1/4 CUP SUGAR
1/2 TSP SALT
1 CUP MILK, SCALDED
3/4 CUP MASHED POTATOES
2 EGGS, BEATEN
4 TO 6 CUPS ALL-PURPOSE FLOUR
VEGETABLE OIL

In a small bowl, dissolve yeast in warm water. In a large
bowl, combine shortening, sugar, salt, and hot milk. Add in
yeast mixture, potatoes, and eggs. Beat well. Mix in flour a
little at a time to make a soft dough. Turn out onto
floured surface and knead well. Place in a large buttered
bowl and let rise in a warm place (preferably 80 degrees)
until double in size, about 1 to 1 1/2 hours. Punch down and
let rest for 10 minutes. Roll dough 1/2-inch thick and cut
with a doughnut cutter.* Let rise until double. In a nice,
heavy, deep skillet, heat oil until 375 degrees and deep fry
doughnuts a few at a time until golden brown. Drain on
paper towels. Glaze (see following recipe) or sprinkle with
powdered sugar.

*There are several alternatives to an actual doughnut
cutter. Try using a glass and then a pop bottle top to cut
out the middle.

Makes 3 1/2 dozen

Glaze

1 1/2 POUNDS (2 CUPS) CONFECTIONER'S SUGAR
1 1/2 TBSPS BUTTER, MELTED
1 1/2 TSPS VANILLA
1 TO 3 TBSPS WARM MILK

In a small bowl, cream together sugar, butter, and
vanilla. Dribble in milk a little at a time until glaze
is the consistency of canned milk. Dip doughnuts
in glaze, let excess drip off, and set out on tray
until glaze is set. (That is, IF you can keep the
admiring crowd away!)

Disappearing Doughnuts

These are so tasty they won't last long enough to cool!

1/2 CUP BUTTER
I CUP SUGAR
2 EGGS
I TSP GRATED LEMON PEEL
4 1/2 CUPS ALL-PURPOSE FLOUR
2 TSPS SALT
2 TSPS BAKING POWDER
2 TSP GROUND NUTMEG
I CUP MILK
COOKING OIL
1/2 CUP POWDERED SUGAR (OPTIONAL)

In a large bowl, cream together butter and sugar. Add eggs and lemon peel, and beat until fluffy. In a separate bowl, sift together the flour, salt, baking powder, and nutmeg. Add to butter mixture, alternating with the milk until well mixed. Turn out on a floured board, roll out to 1/2-inch thickness, and cut with doughnut cutter. Fry in hot (365 degree) oil a few at a time (don't crowd) until light golden brown, about 3 minutes. Drain on paper towels. If you like these sugared, pour powdered sugar in a brown paper bag, drop in a few hot doughnuts at a time, and shake gently. Remove, shaking off excess sugar.

Makes about 2 dozen

Mother's Cinnamon Flop

I CUP SUGAR
2 CUPS ALL-PURPOSE FLOUR
2 TSPS BAKING POWDER
1/8 TSP SALT
2 TBLSPS BUTTER, MELTED
I CUP MILK

Topping:
1/4 CUP BROWN SUGAR, FIRMLY PACKED
I TBLSP GROUND CINNAMON
1/4 CUP BUTTER

Preheat oven to 350 degrees.

In a large bowl, sift together sugar, flour, baking powder, and salt. Add in first 2 tablespoons butter and the milk, stirring until well mixed. Grease a 9 x 13-inch baking dish and pour in batter. In a small bowl, blend together the brown sugar and cinnamon. Sprinkle mixture over batter. Cut remaining butter into small chunks and poke into the batter. As this butter melts, it will form yummy, gooey pockets. Bake for 30 minutes. Serve warm.

Serves 8 to 10

Seconds Please Doughnuts

4 1/4 CUPS ALL-PURPOSE FLOUR
4 TSPS BAKING POWDER
1 TSP GROUND NUTMEG
1/2 TSP SALT
2 EGGS
1 CUP SUGAR
2 TBLSPS MELTED BUTTER
1 CUP MILK
1 TSP VANILLA
COOKING OIL
POWDERED SUGAR

In a large bowl, sift together the flour, baking powder, nutmeg, and salt. In a separate bowl, beat together the eggs and 1 cup sugar until fluffy. Add in butter, milk, and vanilla. Add in the flour mixture all at once, stirring until smooth. Dough will be soft. Turn out dough onto floured board and roll out to 3/4-inch thick. Cut with floured doughnut cutter. Heat oil in deep, heavy pan to 370 degrees and fry doughnuts until golden brown, turning once. Drain on paper towels. Roll doughnuts in powdered sugar.

Makes 2 dozen

Red River Valley Cherry Muffins

1/3 CUP CORN OIL (OR CANOLA)
2 CUPS WATER
1 CUP CRACKED WHEAT CEREAL (AVAILABLE IN HEALTH FOOD DEPARTMENT)
2 1/2 CUPS BREAD FLOUR
1/2 CUP POWDERED MILK
2 1/2 TSPS BAKING POWDER
1 TSP GROUND CINNAMON
3 EGGS, WELL BEATEN
2/3 CUP BROWN SUGAR, WELL PACKED
3/4 CUP DRIED CHERRIES (CRANBERRIES ARE A GOOD ALTERNATIVE)
1/4 CUP HONEY

Preheat oven to 400 degrees.

In a medium saucepan, bring the oil and water to a boil over medium-high heat. Add in the cereal, stirring occasionally, and cook for 2 minutes. Remove from heat and cool. In a medium bowl, combine the cooked cereal with the flour, dry milk, baking powder, cinnamon, eggs, and brown sugar. Stir until well blended. Mixture will be lumpy. Fold in the dried fruit and honey. Grease two 12-section muffin tins or line with papers. Fill each muffin cup 3/4 full and bake for 20 to 25 minutes or until muffins are browned. Serve with butter.

Makes 24 muffins

Brown Betty (Coffee Cake)

3 CUPS BAKING MIX (LIKE BISQUICK)
1/2 CUP SUGAR
1/2 TSP SALT
2 TSPS GROUND CINNAMON, DIVIDED
1/4 TSP GROUND NUTMEG
1/2 CUP MILK
2 EGGS, SLIGHTLY BEATEN
3 TBLSPS VEGETABLE OIL OR MELTED SHORTENING
1 CAN (1 LB., 4 OZ.) APPLE SLICES OR APPLE PIE FILLING
1/2 CUP BROWN SUGAR, PACKED
1/4 CUP BUTTER
1/3 CUP WALNUTS, COARSELY CHOPPED

Preheat oven to 400 degrees.

In a medium bowl, combine together the baking mix, sugar, salt, 1 teaspoon cinnamon, and nutmeg. In a separate bowl, combine together milk, eggs, and oil, and stir into flour mixture. Spread batter in bottom of greased 8 x 12 x 2-inch baking dish. Cover with apple slices. In a small bowl, combine the brown sugar, flour, and second teaspoon cinnamon. Cut in the butter until crumbly. Add in the nuts and sprinkle this topping over the apple filling. Bake for 35 minutes or until lightly brown. Offer sweet cream to pour over.

Serves 12

Bowl 'em Over

Hearty Bars and Cereals

Somehow television and public relations people on Madison Avenue managed to convince us that a plastic bowl with an equally plastic, sugary, preservative-laden cereal was the breakfast of champions. This wasn't always true. Contrary to myth and legend, good cooks of past generations served more than eggs and flapjacks for their family's first meal of the day. They knew how to fill their deep, stoneware bowls with something worth pouring cream over. Served by themselves or alongside a plate of biscuits, these recipes need no cartoon spokesperson to sell their delicious, rib-stickin' rewards.

Amish Cornmeal Mush

1 QUART BOILING WATER
1 QUART COLD WATER
2 CUPS YELLOW CORNMEAL, TRY TO USE THE COARSER ROASTED
  VARIETY
1/2 CUP ALL PURPOSE FLOUR
1 TSP SALT

Take a large, heavy saucepan and pour in the boiling water. In a bowl, combine cornmeal, flour, and salt, and stir into the boiling water. Slowly add in the cold water, stirring constantly to avoid lumps. Cover and cook over very low heat for 1 to 3 hours until mixture is thick. Serve hot with cherry pie filling and cream.

*Pour any leftover mush into a greased loaf pan and refrigerate. The next morning, cut 1/2-inch thick slices and fry in butter. Serve with maple syrup.

Serves 6 to 8

Your Own Breakfast Bars

2 CUPS CRUNCHY PEANUT BUTTER (USE A BRAND THAT'S ALL
   PEANUT BUTTER AND NOT FULL OF SUGAR)
1 1/2 CUPS SUNFLOWER SEEDS
1 CUP RAISINS
1 CUP DATES, PITTED AND CHOPPED
2 TBSPS BREWER'S YEAST
1 CUP POWDERED MILK
1 CUP HONEY
1 CUP ROLLED OATS

Preheat oven to 250 degrees.

In a large bowl, combine peanut butter, sunflower
seeds, raisins, dates, brewer's yeast, milk, honey, and
oats. Pat into 2 large, shallow baking pans and bake
for 1 hour. Cut into bars.

Makes about 2 dozen

Berkeley Health Bars

3 CUPS ROLLED OATS
2 CUPS SESAME SEEDS
2 CUPS SUNFLOWER MEAL
1/2 CUP POPPY SEEDS
1/4 CUP TOASTED SOY POWDER
1/2 CUP DRY LECITHIN
1 CUP TOASTED WHEAT GERM
1 CUP RAISINS
1/4 CUP BREWER'S YEAST FLAKES
1 CUP UNSWEETENED COCONUT, FINELY CHOPPED
1 CUBE BUTTER
1 CUP HONEY
1 TSP VANILLA

Preheat oven to 325 degrees.

In a large bowl, mix together oats, sesame seeds,
sunflower meal, poppy seeds, soy powder, lecithin,
wheat germ, raisins, yeast flakes, and coconut. In a
small saucepan, melt together butter, honey, and
vanilla. Pour this over granola mixture and mix well.
Press into 2 baking pans 9 x 13 x 2 inches. Bake for
about 40 minutes. Cool. Break up with a fork and
store in air tight container. Serve as a snack,
breakfast cereal, or with yogurt.

Makes about 8 cups

Alabama Grits

1 CUP GRITS
4 CUPS BOILING WATER
1 TSP SALT

In a large saucepan, bring the water to a boil and add salt. Slowly stir in the grits, stirring constantly. Cover and reduce the heat. Continue cooking for about 30 to 40 minutes, stirring often.

Variations:

Southerners like grits served with scrambled eggs or a poached egg on top. Another Southern favorite is to cook the grits and grate in 1 cup sharp cheddar or other flavorful cheese over the top.

An alternative is to pack the leftover cheese grits (or simply double your recipe) into a well-greased loaf pan. Chill overnight. Slice 1-inch thick and fry on both sides in butter until lightly browned.

Serves 3 to 4

106

Burgoo

2 CUPS STEEL-CUT OATS
4 CUPS WATER
1 TSP SALT
3 TBLSP BUTTER
1/4 CUP BROWN SUGAR (WHITE IS OKAY)
1/4 CUP RAISINS, DATES, OR CHOPPED FRESH FRUIT

In a medium saucepan, pour oats into water and bring to
a boil. Reduce heat to low and simmer for 15 minutes,
stirring constantly. Remove from heat and stir in salt,
butter, sugar, and fruit. Serve with cream or half and half
with warm scones and honey.

Serves 4

Amber Waves of Granola

3/4 CUP BUTTER (1 1/2 STICKS), UNSALTED
1/2 CUP MILD-FLAVORED HONEY (TRY A LOCAL VARIETY)
1/2 TSP SALT
1 1/2 TSPS VANILLA
4 1/2 CUPS ROLLED OATS (NOT QUICK COOKING AND PREFERABLY
   THE THICK-CUT KIND FROM REO'S MILL)
1 CUP WHEAT GERM
1 CUP UNSWEETENED SHREDDED COCONUT
1 CUP ALMONDS, WHOLE OR HALVED

Preheat oven to 300 degrees.

In a medium saucepan, combine butter, honey, and salt
and cook over medium heat. Stir occasionally until
mixture is warm and well mixed. Take off heat and stir
in vanilla. In a large bowl, mix together the oats, wheat
germ, coconut, and almonds. Pour over the warm
butter mixture and stir (a fat wooden spoon works
best) until all is moistened. Scoop into two 12 1/2 x 8
1/2-inch baking pans and bake until granola is nicely
brown, about 35 to 40 minutes. Stir every 15 minutes
or so to make sure granola browns evenly. Cool pans on
a wire rack. Stir occasionally as it cools so no big lumps
form. Serve with milk if you must, but cream right
from the cow is heavenly. Wonderful sprinkled on top
of ice cream. Will keep for about a week in a closed
container.

Makes 8 cups

To Top it All Off!

Jams, Jellies, and Other Joys

Picture Gramma standing over a hot wood stove, stirring an enormous blue-enameled kettle with a big wooden spoon. The steam has the perfume of strawberries, peaches, or maybe apple butter. Canning jars stand in sparkly rows waiting for the jams, jellies, and preserves the family will relish all year long. In the midst of winter, a homestead wife would bring out one of these jars, pop it open alongside a dish of freshly churned butter, and plunk down a plate stacked with hot biscuits. Yum! Nowadays, slaving over that kettle is no longer necessary with the modern jam and jelly recipes, but the wonderful results — and the compliments — are the same.

Gramma Grace's Grape Conserve

4 POUNDS CONCORD GRAPES
1/4 CUP ORANGE JUICE
1 TBLSP GRATED ORANGE RIND
5 CUPS SUGAR
1/4 TSP SALT
1 CUP SEEDLESS RAISINS
1 CUP WALNUTS, FINELY CHOPPED

Wash grapes and pinch out of skins. Set aside skins. In a large saucepan, cook grape pulp 5 to 8 minutes over low heat to loosen seeds. Press through sieve. Return to pan and stir in orange juice, rind, sugar, salt, and raisins. Stir constantly over low heat until sugar dissolves. Increase heat and boil until conserve thickens, stirring constantly so it won't scorch. Add in grape skins and cook another 5 minutes. Mixture should get very thick. Stir in walnuts and ladle into sterilized jars. Process 10 minutes in boiling water bath.

Makes 8 half-pints

Apple Blossom Sauce

1/2 CUP SUGAR
1 TBLSP CORNSTARCH
1/4 TSP PUMPKIN PIE SPICE
1 CUP APPLE CIDER
1 TBLSP LEMON JUICE
2 TBLSPS BUTTER

In a saucepan, mix together sugar, cornstarch, and spice. Stir in cider and lemon juice. Over medium-high heat, continue stirring until sauce boils and turns thick. Continue boiling for 1 minute more. Remove from heat and stir in butter. Serve warm.

Makes 1 1/2 cups

California Salsa

This salsa goes well with scrambled eggs and cheese omelets.

8 TO 10 LARGE RIPE TOMATOES, PEELED AND CHOPPED
2 LARGE ONIONS, CHOPPED
4 TO 5 SWEET YELLOW BELL PEPPERS, CHOPPED
2 CANS DICED MILD GREEN CHILE PEPPERS
1/2 CUP APPLE CIDER VINEGAR
1 CAN (6 OZ.) TOMATO SAUCE
2 LARGE CLOVES GARLIC, CHOPPED
2 TSP CHILE POWDER
2 TBLSPS FRESH CILANTRO, CHOPPED
1/2 TSP OREGANO

In a large, non-corrosive canning kettle, combine tomatoes, onions, bell peppers, chile peppers, vinegar, tomato sauce, garlic, chile powder, cilantro, and oregano. Bring to a gentle boil, stirring often, and continue cooking for 30 minutes. Remove from heat and ladle into sterilized canning jars. Process in boiling water bath for 15 minutes.

Makes about 8 pint jars

Loo-zee-anna Yam Jam

2 CUPS COOKED YAMS, SIEVED
2 CUPS APPLE JUICE
3 TBLSPS LEMON JUICE
1/2 TSP CINNAMON
1/2 TSP ALLSPICE
1/4 TSP GROUND CLOVES
2 TBLSPS HONEY

In a large saucepot or enameled kettle, combine yams, apple and lemon juices, cinnamon, allspice, and cloves. Simmer over medium heat for about 10 minutes. Reduce heat to low and continue cooking until mixture thickens to the consistency of apple butter, about 1 1/2 to 2 hours. Stir often. Remove from heat and stir in honey. Ladle into hot, sterilized jars and process in boiling water bath for 10 minutes. Can be stored in refrigerator for up to a week.

Makes about 2 half-pint jars

Beach Bunny Marmalade

4 POUNDS RAW CARROTS, PEELED
3 LEMONS
2 CUPS CANNED, CRUSHED PINEAPPLE
4 CUPS SUGAR
1 CUP ORANGE JUICE

Put carrots and lemons through food processor. Leave peel on lemons. Pour into a large saucepan with the pineapple, sugar, and orange juice. Cook until clear, stirring occasionally. Pour into hot jars and seal with lids. Process in boiling water bath for 10 minutes.

Makes 4 half-pint jars

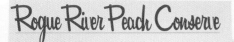

Rogue River Peach Conserve

4 CUPS PEACHES, PEELED AND DICED
1/4 CUP LEMON JUICE
1 TBLSP GRATED LEMON RIND
1 PACKAGE (3 OZ.) PECTIN
6 CUPS SUGAR
1/4 CUP MARASCHINO CHERRIES, CHOPPED
1/2 CUP NUTS, CHOPPED (WALNUTS TASTE BEST.)

In a large, heavy kettle, combine peaches, lemon juice, pectin, and lemon rind. Bring to a hard boil and boil for 4 minutes. Stir in cherries and nuts. Remove from heat, skim off any foam and stir for 5 minutes. Ladle into sterilized jars and process in boiling water bath for 10 minutes.

Makes about 6 pints.

Angelwing Jam

2 MEDIUM ORANGES, UNPEELED
1 LEMON, UNPEELED
2 CUPS COLD WATER
6 MEDIUM PEACHES, PEELED, CORED, AND DICED
6 MEDIUM PEARS, PEELED, CORED, AND DICED
6 MEDIUM APPLES, PEELED, CORED, AND DICED
SUGAR
2 CUPS CANNED, CRUSHED PINEAPPLE

Grind oranges and lemon in food processor. Pour into a large, enameled kettle and cover with cold water; let stand overnight. In the morning, bring mixture to a boil over medium-high heat and cook until tender. Add peaches, pears, and apples to citrus mixture. Measure the total and return to kettle. Add an equal amount of sugar. Add in pineapple. Bring to a gentle boil and continue cooking until mixture thickens, about 30 minutes. Stir often. Ladle into sterilized jars and process in boiling water bath for 10 to 15 minutes.

Makes 4 to 5 pints

Prairie Rose Cherry Jam

3 1/2 CUPS FRESH, PITTED SOUR CHERRIES, CHOPPED (LIKE
    MONTMORENCY, METEOR, OR NORTH STAR)
4 1/2 CUPS SUGAR
1/2 CUP AMARETTO LIQUEUR
3 OZ. LIQUID PECTIN

In a large kettle, combine cherries, sugar, and
amaretto. Bring to a rolling boil over high heat,
stirring constantly. Boil for 1 minute. Remove
from heat and stir in pectin. Skin off any foam
and ladle mixture into sterilized jars. Process for
10 minutes in boiling water bath.

Makes 6 half-pint jars

Pikeville Peach/Plum Jam

4 CUPS FRESH PEACHES, WASHED, PEELED, PITTED AND CHOPPED
5 CUPS FRESH SWEET RED PLUMS, WASHED, PEELED, PITTED AND CHOPPED
1 FRESH LEMON, ENDS CUT OFF, THINLY SLICED
8 CUPS SUGAR

Place peaches, plums, and lemon slices in a large canning kettle. Add in sugar and stir well. Bring to a rolling boil, stirring constantly so jam doesn't scorch. Continue boiling until mixture thickens, about 20 minutes.* Remove from heat and skim off any foam. (Kids love this on fresh homemade biscuits or bread!) Ladle into sterilized jars and process 10 minutes in a boiling water bath.

*As an alternative, follow directions on the package for making peach jam with products like Sure-Jell.

Makes 12 half-pint jars

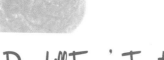

Downhill Farm's Tomato Preserves

5 POUNDS FIRM, RIPE TOMATOES (YOU CAN USE THOSE SWEET
   LITTLE YELLOW PEAR ONES, TOO)
5 POUNDS SUGAR
1 FRESH LEMON, SLICED VERY THIN
1 TSP GROUND GINGER

Dip tomatoes in boiling water for 5 to 10 seconds, cool in ice water. Remove from water, peel (the peels should slip right off), and chop. Pour into a large kettle and add in sugar, lemon, and ginger. Simmer over low heat until thick, about 45 minutes to an hour. Pour into hot jars and seal with lids. Process in boiling water bath for 10 minutes.

Makes about 4 pints

Tillie's Golden Marmalade

8 CUPS CARROTS, PEELED AND GRATED
1 TSP GROUND GINGER
4 CUPS HONEY (SHOULD BE A LIGHT-COLORED
VARIETY LIKE CLOVER OR WILDFLOWER)
2 TBLSPS LEMON JUICE

In a large bowl, mix together the carrots, ginger, and honey. Let sit overnight in a cool place. Spoon into a large kettle and simmer over very low heat for 1 1/2 to 2 hours. The carrots should be transparent. Ladle into sterilized canning jars and process for 10 minutes in a boiling water bath.

Makes 8 half-pint jars

Cranberry Jelly

2 CUPS FRESH CRANBERRIES,
WASHED AND PICKED OVER
1/2 CUP WATER
3/4 CUP SUGAR

In a medium saucepan, simmer cranberries and water until the berries pop. Press berries through a sieve. Add the sugar. Cook for 3 to 5 minutes. Chill until jelly thickens. Serve as you would any other jelly.

Makes 1 cup

Easy Apple Butter

2 QUARTS WATER
1 TBLSP SALT
6 POUNDS APPLES, CORED PEELED AND SLICED (TRY A
  COMBINATION OF SWEET AND TART.)
2 QUARTS SWEET CIDER
4 CUPS SUGAR
1 TSP CINNAMON
1/2 TSP ALLSPICE
1/2 TSP CLOVES

Preheat oven to 350 degrees.

In a large kettle pour in water; add in salt and
apples. Cover and simmer on low for 30 minutes
or until soft. Drain well. Put apples through food
processor or chop by hand. There should be 2
quarts of apples and their juice. Combine with
cider and place in a large enamel pan. Simmer in
center of oven for about 3 to 3 1/2 hours until
apple mixture is cooked down by about half and
is soft. In a separate bowl combine sugar,
cinnamon, allspice, and cloves. Return to pan
and continue baking another 1 1/2 hours or until
thick. Stir about every half hour to avoid
sticking. Test by spooning a little on a saucer. If
no liquid seeps around edges, it's done. Ladle
into hot jars. Place on sterilized lids and screw
tight with bands. Process, while still hot, in a
boiling water bath for 10 minutes.

Makes 4 pints

Topeka Corncob Jelly

12 BRIGHT RED CORNCOBS (CHECK OUT YOUR LOCAL
  FARMER'S MARKET)
3 PINTS WATER
1 PACKAGE PECTIN, SUCH AS SURE-JELL
3 CUPS SUGAR

Break the cobs into several pieces and
boil in water for 30 minutes. Remove and
strain out the liquid, reserving 3 cups.
Add water if needed, pour into a
medium saucepan, and stir in pectin.
Bring to a rolling boil. Add sugar, stirring
well, and boil another 2 or 3 minutes.
Pour into sterilized half-pint jars and
process according to pectin directions.

Makes 6 half-pint jars

Crystal Pear Preserves

2 QUARTS PEARS, PEELED, CORED, SLICED THIN
6 CUPS SUGAR
2 TBLSPS LEMON JUICE
1 TBLSP GRATED LEMON RIND
1 CUP CRYSTALLIZED GINGER, CHOPPED (1 TBSP
　 GROUND GINGER MAY BE USED INSTEAD)

In a large stockpot or canning kettle, place pears and sugar and mix well. Let stand in a cool place overnight. The next day, add lemon juice, rind, and ginger. Bring to a boil, stirring occasionally. Reduce heat to low and simmer until pears turn clear, about 2 hours. Mixture should be thick. Ladle into sterilized jars, seal, and process in boiling water bath for 10 minutes. Can also be frozen.

Makes 8 half-pint jars

Blushing Apple Jelly

5 POUNDS (15 CUPS) TART, RED-SKINNED APPLES
10 CUPS WATER
6 CUPS APPLE JUICE
4 CUPS SUGAR

Cut out stem and blossom ends of apple, but do not peel or core. In a large canning kettle, simmer apples with water until apples are tender. Scoop cooked apples into a jelly bag or cheesecloth and hang so juice will drip into a bowl. This takes several hours or overnight. The next day, measure 6 cups of juice into a kettle and bring to a boil. Stir in sugar and continue boiling until mixture reaches jelling stage (220 to 222 degrees). Another method of testing is to dip a metal spoon into jelly and hold it on edge over a plate. If jelly forms a sheet it's thick enough. Scoop off any foam and pour immediately into sterilized jars. Process in boiling water bath for 10 minutes.

Makes 6 pint jars

Sunshine Jelly

1 PACKAGE (4 OZ.) FRUIT PECTIN
2 CUPS LUKEWARM WATER
1 (6 OZ.) CAN FROZEN ORANGE JUICE CONCENTRATE
1/4 CUP FRESH LEMON JUICE
4 1/2 CUPS SUGAR, DIVIDED

In a medium bowl, dissolve pectin in the luke-warm water, stirring constantly. Let sit for 45 minutes, stirring occasionally. Thaw orange juice and pour with lemon juice into a medium bowl. Add in 2 1/2 cups sugar and stir until mostly dissolved. Add the remaining 2 cups sugar to pectin mixture and stir until dissolved. Combine juice and pectin mixtures and stir well. Pour into freezer containers and let stand overnight or until set. Freeze or refrigerate.

Makes about 6 half-pint jars

Maple Spread

1 CUP REAL MAPLE SYRUP
3/4 CUP BUTTER

In a heavy-bottomed saucepan, heat syrup until it reaches the soft-ball candy stage (235 to 250 degrees). Add in butter and stir until it melts. Pour in a deep bowl and beat with an electric mixer until spread is thick and creamy.

Makes 1 3/4 cups.

Peach Butter

1/2 CUP BUTTER
1/2 CUP PEACH PRESERVES
1/4 TSP NUTMEG

In a small bowl, whip together butter, preserves, and nutmeg until fluffy.

Makes 1 cup.

Index